W9-BPS-091

THE FLAMES OF WAR

THE FIGHT FOR UPPER CANADA, JULY–DECEMBER 1813

UPPER CANADA PRESERVED
WAR OF 1812

THE FLAMES OF WAR

THE FIGHT FOR UPPER CANADA,
JULY–DECEMBER 1813

RICHARD FELTOE

DUNDURN
TORONTO

Copyright © Richard Feltoe, 2013

All rights reserved. No part of this publication may be reproduced, stored in a retrieval system, or transmitted in any form or by any means, electronic, mechanical, photocopying, recording, or otherwise (except for brief passages for purposes of review) without the prior permission of Dundurn Press. Permission to photocopy should be requested from Access Copyright.

Editor: Cheryl Hawley
Design: Jennifer Scott
Printer: Webcom

Library and Archives Canada Cataloguing in Publication

Feltoe, Richard, 1954-
The flames of war : the fight for Upper Canada, July--December 1813 / by Richard Feltoe.

(Upper Canada preserved War of 1812)
Includes bibliographical references and index.
Issued also in electronic formats.
ISBN 978-1-4597-0702-3

1. Canada--History--War of 1812. 2. Canada--History--War of 1812--Campaigns. 3. Canada--History--War of 1812--Battlefields. I. Title. II. Series: Feltoe, Richard, 1954- . Upper Canada preserved War of 1812.

FC442.F425 2013   971.03'4   C2012-907682-1

1   2   3   4   5   17   16   15   14   13

  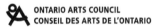

We acknowledge the support of the Canada Council for the Arts and the Ontario Arts Council for our publishing program. We also acknowledge the financial support of the Government of Canada through the Canada Book Fund and Livres Canada Books, and the Government of Ontario through the Ontario Book Publishing Tax Credit and the Ontario Media Development Corporation.

Care has been taken to trace the ownership of copyright material used in this book. The author and the publisher welcome any information enabling them to rectify any references or credits in subsequent editions.

J. Kirk Howard, President

Printed and bound in Canada.

Unless otherwise attributed, images and maps are the property and copyright of the author.

Visit us at
Dundurn.com | Definingcanada.ca | @dundurnpress | Facebook.com/dundurnpress

Dundurn	Gazelle Book Services Limited	Dundurn
3 Church Street, Suite 500	White Cross Mills	2250 Military Road
Toronto, Ontario, Canada	High Town, Lancaster, England	Tonawanda, NY
M5E 1M2	LA1 4XS	U.S.A. 14150

This book is offered:

First, as a salute to the memory of all those, on both sides of the lines, who served, sacrificed, and died as they loyally obeyed their country's call-to-arms in the North American War of 1812–1815.

Second, as a mark of respect to the men and women of the military services of Canada, Great Britain, and the United States, who today honorably continue that legacy of service and sacrifice at home and across the globe.

Third, as a thank-you to my fellow "Living History" reenactors, with and against whom I've "fought" for so many years.

Finally, as a memory from "Bamp" to my grandsons, Anthony, Lawrence, and Daniel.

TABLE OF CONTENTS

ACKNOWLEDGEMENTS

To completely misquote the famous saying "Never has so much been owed by one to so many" may be mangling history, but it is true nonetheless. This series cannot be considered the product of myself alone, but rests upon the work and studies of countless individuals over the past 200 years, who preserved the original letters and documents or wrote the stories of the War of 1812–1815 for me to review and learn from. As such, I can only hope to assure all those who have gone before, and who in recent years have directly given me their support and encouragement, that their efforts are deeply and gratefully appreciated but page space forbids their individual mention. Therefore, I must restrict myself to naming and thanking but a few, whilst saluting the many.

To my wife, Diane, who has become my "manager" when it comes to public speaking and promotional engagements, book signings, marketing opportunities, communications, stock management, and accounting, thanks for putting up with all of this. Three down, halfway there … until the next ones.

To my friend and fellow historian Pat Kavanagh, whose generosity in providing me unrestricted access to his vast resource collection of American records, official documents, and personal letters on the war revealed a treasure trove of historical information, my respect and gratitude.

To one of Canada's current leading historical authors, Donald Graves, I deem it a privilege to have been able to work alongside and exchange information with you and to learn from a master on the value of our heritage.

To the many dedicated staff members of the numerous museums, archives, and libraries that I visited to undertake the research for this work, and who cheerfully assisted my searches to fruition, your dedication and expertise is a national treasure that cannot be measured or underestimated.

Penultimately, I cannot fail to acknowledge the continued guidance and support provided by my editor, Cheryl Hawley, my designer, Jennifer Scott, as well as the whole creative team at Dundurn Press in turning this idea into a reality.

Finally, to the memory of Karen, for her determination to see me do a proper job of telling the story now being presented here.

Thank you!
Richard Feltoe

PREFACE

VARIATIONS

As more fully outlined in the introduction to the first part of this series, the historic material included here includes variations in spelling, jargon, and place name changes that have occurred over time. As a result, the following standards have been applied:

- Where variations on spelling in quotes are found, the material has been repeatedly checked to ensure its accuracy and is presented just as it was found in the original documents and without the term [*sic*].
- While generally recognized military terms are presented as is, some of the more archaic or jargon-type words are either followed by a modern equivalent word or referenced in a separate glossary of terms. In a similar manner, maintaining the differential identification of military units from the two principal combatant nations (when both used a system of numbers to designate their regiments) has been achieved by showing British Regimental numbers as numerals (41st Regiment, 89th Regiment, etc.) and where required with their subsidiary titles (1st [Royal Scots] Regiment, 8th [King's] Regiment), whilst the American Regiments are expressed as words (First Regiment, Twenty-Fifth Regiment, etc.).
- Where place names appear with a number of variants (e.g., Sackett's Harbour, Sacket's Harbour, Sakets Harbor, or Sacket's Harbor) I have adopted a single format for each case, based upon a judgment of what I felt was

the predominant version used at the time. Where names have changed entirely, or would cause needless confusion (Newark becoming Niagara and currently Niagara-on-the-Lake), I have generally gone with what would clarify the location and simplify identification overall or included a reference to the modern name (Crossroads becoming Virgil).

Finally, in including images where there is both a period and modern image combined for a then-and-now effect, I have tried, as far as possible, to obtain the same relative perspective — subject to the limitations imposed where the physical landscape and property ownership make it possible to do so.

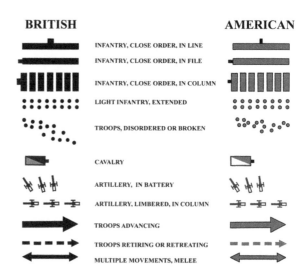

BRITISH		AMERICAN
	INFANTRY, CLOSE ORDER, IN LINE	
	INFANTRY, CLOSE ORDER, IN FILE	
	INFANTRY, CLOSE ORDER, IN COLUMN	
	LIGHT INFANTRY, EXTENDED	
	TROOPS, DISORDERED OR BROKEN	
	CAVALRY	
	ARTILLERY, IN BATTERY	
	ARTILLERY, LIMBERED, IN COLUMN	
	TROOPS ADVANCING	
	TROOPS RETIRING OR RETREATING	
	MULTIPLE MOVEMENTS, MELEE	

THE FLAMES OF WAR

THE FIGHT FOR UPPER CANADA,
JULY–DECEMBER 1813

CHAPTER 1

Introduction

On June 18, 1812, the United States declared war on Great Britain with the expectation that it would soon gain an easy victory and occupy Britain's colonies of Upper and Lower Canada. Unfortunately, the initial months of the war went badly wrong for the American cause, as they then lost a succession of battles to an alliance of British regular troops, Canadian militia forces, and Native allied warriors (hereafter, Allied forces).

During early 1813, these embarrassments continued at Frenchtown and Ogdensburg. However, by the spring, a reorganized American war effort gained the desired military victories at York (Toronto) and Newark (Niagara-on-the-Lake), though only at a significant cost in casualties to the invasion force. Occupying the Niagara River frontier, the Americans forced the British to retreat to the Head-of-the-Lake (Hamilton), but the momentum of the invasion was reversed by the Allied surprise night attack at Stoney Creek. By the end of June 1813, the American army on the Niagara had been herded into a militarized enclave at Newark in order to defend themselves against a renewed Allied offensive.

The details of this period of the war can be found in the first two books in this six-part series, *The Call to Arms* and *The Pendulum of War*. This work, *The Flames of War*, now takes up that story in order to trace the course of the conflict during the final six months of 1813 on the "Northern" frontier. For those who have not read the two previous works, the following timeline should provide a background to the events immediately prior to the events described in this work.

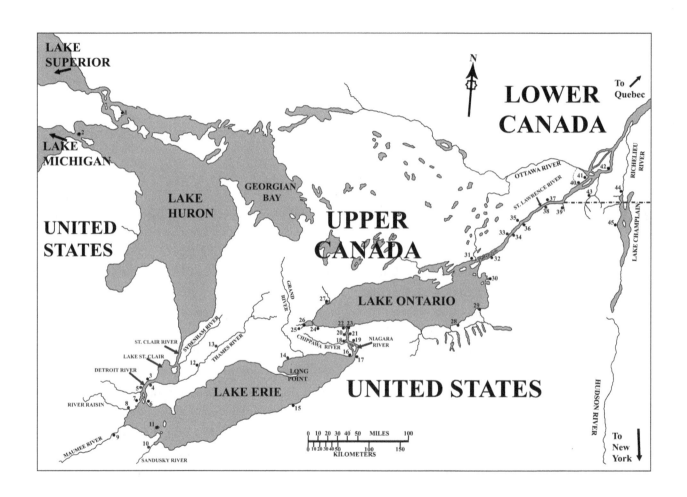

THE "NORTHERN FRONTIER" OF THE WAR OF 1812–1815.

(Modern Name)   [Fortifications]

1. St. Joseph Island [Fort St. Joseph]
2. Michilimackinac Island (Mackinac) [Fort Mackinac/Fort Michilimackinac]
3. Detroit [Fort Detroit]
4. Sandwich (Windsor)
5. Monguagon/Maguaga
6. Amherstburg (Malden) [Fort Amherstburg]
7. Brownstown
8. Frenchtown
9. Perrysburg [Fort Meigs]
10. [Fort Stephenson]
11. Put-in-Bay
12. Moravianstown
13. Longwoods
14. Port Dover
15. Presque Isle (Erie, PA)
16. Fort Erie [Fort Erie]
17. Buffalo and Black Rock
18. Chippawa
19. [Fort Schlosser]
20. Queenston
21. Lewiston
22. Newark (Niagara-on-the-Lake) [Fort George, Fort Mississauga]
23. [Fort Niagara]
24. Stoney Creek
25. Ancaster
26. Burlington Heights (Hamilton, ON)
27. York (Toronto) [Fort York]
28. Sodus
29. Oswego [Fort Oswego]
30. Sackets Harbor [Fort Tompkins, Fort Volunteer, Fort Pike]
31. Kingston [Fort Frederick, Fort Henry]
32. French Creek
33. Elizabethtown/ Brockville (1813)
34. Morrisburg
35. Prescott [Fort Wellington]
36. Ogdensburg
37. Crysler's Farm
38. Hamilton (Waddington, NY)
39. French Mills
40. Coteau-du-Lac
41. Cedars
42. Montreal
43. Châteauguay
44. Île aux Noix
45. Plattsburg

TIMELINE OF EVENTS

- April 27, 1813: [Upper Canada] The Battle of York (Toronto). The American s defeat the Allied forces defending York (Toronto). As they retreat, the British explode their main magazine, inflicting heavy casualties on the American forces. In retaliation, the Americans burn the town's public buildings (Parliament) and Fort York.

- May 27, 1813: [Niagara frontier] The Battle of Fort George. American forces defeat the Allied forces in heavy fighting around Newark (Niagara-on-the-Lake). The Allied forces are forced to abandon Fort George and retreat to Burlington Heights/Head-of-the-Lake (Hamilton).

- May 1–9, 1813: [Detroit frontier] The Siege of Fort Meigs. General Proctor mounts an Allied pre-emptive campaign to destroy the new American fortification of Fort Meigs. Although the siege fails, the expedition cripples the American plans to mount a counter invasion for several months to come.

- May 29, 1813: [Lake Ontario] Battle of Sackets Harbor. Allied forces mount an amphibious attack on the American naval base at Sackets Harbor. Despite defeating all American opposition, causing the fleeing Americans to begin destroying their own positions and naval warehouses, the senior British commander, Sir

PERSONALITIES RELATED TO THE WAR

1. Sir George Prevost (commander in chief, British Forces, and governor general, British North America).
By S.W. Reynolds, date unknown, Library and Archives Canada, C-1912.

2. James Madison (U.S. president).
Courtesy of the Buffalo and Erie County Historical Society Research Library, Buffalo, NY.

3. John Armstrong (U.S. secretary of war).
Courtesy of the Buffalo and Erie County Historical Society Research Library, Buffalo, NY.

4. Major General James Wilkinson (U.S. senior commander, "Great Lakes").
Courtesy of the Buffalo and Erie County Historical Society Research Library, Buffalo, NY.

5. Commodore Isaac Chauncey (U.S. naval commander, "Northern frontier").
Library and Archives Canada, C-010926.

6. Colonel Winfield Scott.
Courtesy of the Buffalo and Erie County Historical Society Research Library, Buffalo, NY.

7. Tecumseh (Leaping Panther).
From *Pictorial Field Book of the War of 1812.*

8. Sir James Yeo (British senior naval commander, "Great Lakes").
From *Pictorial Field Book of the War of 1812.*

George Prevost, orders the abandonment of the attack.

- June 6, 1813: [Niagara frontier] The Battle of Stoney Creek. Allied forces make a surprise night attack on the Americans encamped at Stoney Creek. Following a confused and disorganized melee, both sides conclude they have lost the engagement and mutually retreat. However, during the following days, the American invasion collapses and the Americans retreat to a militarized enclave around Fort George/Newark, while abandoning their occupied posts at Fort Erie and Chippawa.

- June 24, 1813: [Niagara frontier] The Battle of Beaver Dams. American forces being besieged at Fort George attempt a large-scale sortie to disrupt the Allied positions at Beaver Dams. Lax security while on the march allows Laura Secord to bring word to the Allied forces, who use their Native allies to entrap and defeat the American sortie.

CHAPTER 2

Striking While the Iron Is Hot: *The Niagara Frontier, July–August 1813*

With the American war efforts stalled on the Detroit frontier and thrown onto the defensive on the Niagara frontier, the British command, emboldened by their recent successes, decided to move back onto the offensive. Unfortunately the new British military commander for Upper Canada, Major General Baron Francis de Rottenburg, did not have the same depth of understanding as his predecessor, Major General Brock, about the significance of maintaining and enhancing the military alliances that had been forged between the British regulars, the Canadian militia, and Native allied warriors. He also effectively disregarded the crucial role the Natives had played in preserving Upper Canada during its darkest hours at the outset of the war. Instead, he saw the efforts of Colonel Henry Proctor to fight his campaigns on the Detroit frontier and the Upper Lakes as a far distant and only a marginally important campaign front, while the huge amount of supplies and gifts provided to the Native allied tribes each year were an inconvenient and unnecessary drain on his limited military and civilian resources. On the other hand, the recent military victories on the Niagara frontier were far more immediate in geographical proximity, ease of supply, and in his mind, military importance. To this end, de Rottenburg concentrated his efforts and resources where he believed they would have the most significant effect and prove of most value.

During the initial days of what may be referred to as the siege of Fort George, (although it actually encompassed a much wider area than that single fortification) the Allied forces not only maintained a

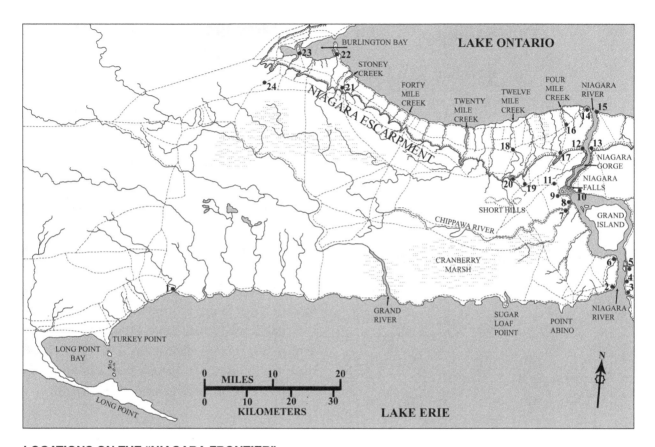

LOCATIONS ON THE "NIAGARA FRONTIER"

1. Port Dover
2. Fort Erie [Fort Erie]
3. Buffalo
4. Black Rock
5. U.S. Naval Yard on Scajaquada Creek
6. Frenchman's Creek
7. Weishoun's
8. [Fort Chippawa]
9. Bridgewater Mills
10. Fort Schlosser
11. Lundy's Lane Hilltop
12. Queenston
13. Lewiston
14. Newark (Niagara-on-the-Lake) [Fort George, Fort Mississauga]
15. [Fort Niagara]
16. Crossroads (Virgil)
17. St. Davids
18. Shipman's Corners (St. Catharines)
19. Beaver Dams
20. De Cou (DeCew) Mill
21. Stoney Creek
22. King's Head Inn
23. Burlington Heights (Hamilton)
24. Ancaster

Locations along the Niagara River.

steady series of probing attacks against the American outlying pickets, they also actively went on the offensive, as exampled by the sortie made by a party of thirty-four local 2nd Lincoln Militia (Lieutenant Colonel Thomas Clark) and supported by six regulars from the 49th Regiment (Ensign Winder).[1] Crossing the Niagara River at dawn on July 5th, they quickly overpowered a small guard detachment of eleven men and captured the American supply base at Fort Schlosser, without a shot being fired. Ransacking the depot, they returned to their own side of the river, carrying off a significant amount of valuable supplies.

A few days later, a more ambitious foray took place at Black Rock, just downstream from Buffalo. There, a planned small-scale raid was enlarged into a major operation against the U.S. naval repair yard, warehouses, and battery defences lining the American side of the river around Black Rock.

The Battle of Black Rock, July 11, 1813

At around 2:00 a.m. on July 11th, a combined force of about 250 men, drawn from the 8th (King's), 41st, and 49th regular regiments, and the 2nd/3rd Lincoln Embodied Militia, used the cover of a heavy fog to cross the Niagara River undetected. Their goal was to land just below the Scajaquada Creek, where the American naval yard was located.[*2] However, the

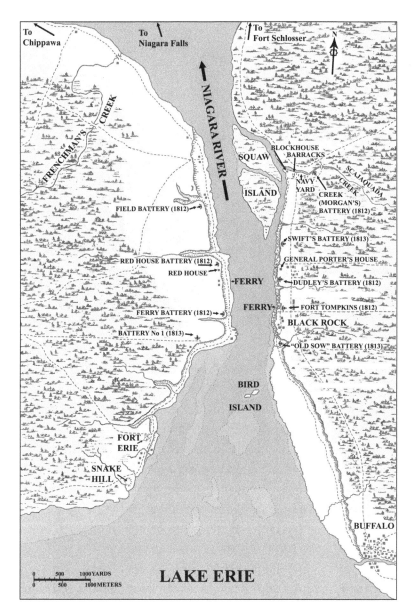

swift river current scattered the boats, so that only Lieutenant Fitzgibbon's 49th in the advance guard landed near to their assigned location, while the remainder of the boats beached along two miles of the riverbank. With daylight approaching, Fitzgibbon's party pressed ahead without waiting for Lieutenant Colonel Bisshopp and his main force to arrive.

THE RAID ON BLACK ROCK, JULY 11, 1813[2]

British

Royal Artillery (Lieutenant Armstrong) 20 gunners
8th (Kings) Regiment (Lieutenant Barstow) 40 rank and file
41st Regiment (Captain Saunders) 100 rank and file
49th Regiment (Lieutenant Fitzgibbon) 40 rank and file
2nd/3rd Lincoln Militia (Lieutenant Colonel Clark) 40 rank and file
Total: 240 rank and file, plus officers, boat crews, etc. Estimated 350 all ranks.

Left: Military positions around Buffalo/Black Rock/Fort Erie in July 1813.

Reaching the bridge over the creek, they found it guarded by a single sentry who fled without firing a shot. As a result, the nearby shipyard garrison was surprised and overwhelmed within minutes. Following the arrival of the main body of troops, detachments were assigned to strip the warehouses before setting fire to the shipyard. At the same time, under the continued cover of the fog, the rest of the main column successively overran each of the American batteries lining the riverbank, eventually they approached within a hundred yards (91 meters) of the main American militia encampment and adjacent battery position at Black Rock. At this point, the alarm was finally raised by the startled American sentries. Uncertain how many troops were manning the post, Bisshopp pushed his luck and demanded the garrison's immediate surrender. Upon hearing this call, while the American officers deliberated their response, their men made their position clear, to a man, by abandoning their guns, scrambling over the front wall of the battery position, and disappearing off into the fog. The British also nearly captured Brigadier General Peter B. Porter, who was in bed as the British arrived at his headquarters, forcing the general to decamp in a hurry — reportedly dressed only in his nightshirt, and leaving his horse behind for the subsequent use of Lieutenant Colonel Bisshopp. Having overwhelmed the entire Black Rock garrison without

Brigadier General Peter B. Porter.

Courtesy of the Buffalo and Erie County Historical Society Research Library, Buffalo, NY.

losing a single man, Bisshopp's troops spiked the heavier battery guns and expropriated two field pieces. They also transferred the contents of the adjacent warehouses into several captured bateaux, which became overloaded and were in danger of sinking. Assigning a number of the militiamen to act as crews, Bisshopp sent the heavily laden boats over to Fort Erie as prizes of war.

With the principal objective of the raid achieved, and in full daylight, Lieutenant Colonel Bisshopp ordered his troops to withdraw toward General Porter's house, where they were to rendezvous with their waiting transport. Behind them, columns of smoke marked the various structures and fortifications around Black Rock. The British also set fire to a fully loaded cargo schooner that had fallen into their hands, because there was no crew to sail it. The British troops were almost finished re-embarking their boats when they came under a heavy fire from the nearby woods. This counterattack was made up of some 300 American regular and militia troops that had been gathered together by General Porter, supported by a number of Seneca Native allies who, for the first time, were actively engaging in combat on behalf of the United States. Composed of elements of the Black Rock garrison, relief forces from Buffalo, and detachments of volunteers, this force had been divided into three wings by General Porter with a plan of simultaneously attacking the British on three sides.[*3] However, due to a delay within Major King's central force (which some accounts claim was the result of a disagreement between two senior officers over who was to command the attack), only the two wings undertook the initial assault. Nevertheless, the American shooting caught the unprepared British in a devastating crossfire on the exposed riverbank. Hastily forming a defensive perimeter in order to allow the majority of the boats to escape, the last boats were loaded and attempted to pull out of range as British casualties in the rearguard mounted.

Because the last boat contained a large number of wounded men, including Lieutenant Colonel Bisshopp, it was initially unable to propel itself out of range and was nearly captured by some of the American Native allies who "plunged into the water, seized upon the gunnels of the boat, and would have brought it to shore, but from the fire from the rear, which obliged them to desist."[4] Drifting downriver, the boat was pursued by the Americans, demanding that its crew come ashore and surrender. Pleading they had too many casualties to comply, the boat continued to drift until it reached Squaw Island, whereupon the crew "miraculously"

THE RAID ON BLACK ROCK, JULY 11, 1813[*3]

American Counterattack

Centre Division: 100 rank and file, regulars (Captain Cummings, superseded by Major King as the action commenced), and 30 local volunteers (Captain Hull)

Left Division: 150 rank and file, Genesee Militia (Major Adams)

Right Division: 30 rank and file, Plains Militia Volunteers (Captain Bull), and 30 Native warriors (Farmer's Brother)

Total Force: 300–325 all ranks

healed and began pulling as hard as they could out into the mainstream. Enraged at being fooled, the Americans again opened fire, only to see the boat slip away behind the cover of the island, effectively ending the American pursuit and the battle.[*5]

Although subsequent British reports characterized the action as a glowing success, the wounding of

The grave of Lieutenant Colonel Cecil Bisshopp (written as Bishopp on the tombstone) in the Drummond Hill cemetery at Lundy's Lane (Niagara Falls).

OFFICIAL ESTIMATES OF CASUALTIES, RAID ON BLACK ROCK, JULY 11, 1813[*5]

British Regulars and Canadian Militias

Killed:	1 officer, 13 rank and file
Wounded:	5 officers, 1 sergeant, 20 rank and file
Missing/Prisoner:	1 officer, 6 rank and file

(N.B. American accounts refer to capturing at least 16 all ranks, while upon their return civilian prisoners claimed that the British had acknowledged at least 100 killed, wounded, and missing from the attack.)

American Regulars and Militias

Killed:	4 all ranks
Wounded:	5 all ranks
Prisoner:	6 all ranks, 4 civilians

American Native Allies

Wounded:	2 warriors

Lieutenant Colonel Bisshopp proved mortal within a few days, depriving the British forces on the Niagara of a popular and able commander. In addition, because de Rottenburg had chosen to make the expedition using detachments of the 41st Regiment, troops that had been previously destined for Amherstburg by Sir George Prevost's direct instruction, it denied these vital resources to General Proctor at a time when his military situation was rapidly progressing from difficult to desperate.

From the American perspective, the destruction of their defences at Black Rock and, more importantly, the loss of the large stockpiles of food, equipment, and ammunition, precipitated a crisis of supply — not only for the garrisons at Black Rock and Buffalo, but also for the besieged American troops at Fort George. Conversely, it supplemented the rapidly diminishing British reserves, as there was no sign of Yeo's fleet arriving with fresh supplies and reinforcements of men.

One additional and unexpected consequence of this action was that the voluntary commitment and involvement of the small detachment of American Native allies, seen to be fighting alongside the "white" American troops, encouraged other tribes along that side of the Niagara to step forward and offer to fight for the United States. With the encouragement (and literary assistance) of some of their white associates, they were also persuaded to issue a declaration of war against Upper and Lower Canada.

> We, the Chiefs and Counsellors of the Six Nations of Indians, residing in the State of New York, do hereby proclaim to all the War Chiefs and Warriors of the Six Nations that War is declared on our part upon the Provinces of Upper and Lower Canada. Therefore, we do command and advise all the War Chiefs to call forth immediately their warriors under them and put them in motion to protect their rights and liberties which our brethren the Americans are now defending.

> Signed by the Grand Councillors.[6]
> — *Utica Patriot*, August 24, 1813

Within days, over one hundred warriors had volunteered to fight. In response, General Porter decided, without consulting his government, to enrol these volunteers into a company of the army. War chiefs were granted "commissions" as captains, lieutenants, and ensigns. As might be expected, this unapproved enrollment was not received well by the Washington administration and Porter found himself privately censured for his initiative. Similarly, at the field level, the concept of Natives holding official ranks was rejected out of hand by the majority of white regular and militia officers. Even the very offer of Native warriors fighting for the American cause was met with a wave of contempt by many American commanders, who derided the Native methods of fighting and demanded that any warrior volunteers submit themselves to being commanded exclusively by white officers. This insult and subsequent lack of flexibility in dealing with these proud and independent warriors escalated tensions to the point where certain American officers refused to bring their troops to the aid of the Natives when they were pressed in battle. In addition, some openly claimed that these American Native allies were being deliberately used as a bargaining ploy to persuade the British to stop using their own Natives in battle. Inevitably, after several weeks of being used as "cannon fodder" many warriors quit the front in disgust, while those who did remain made it quite clear that their further co-operation depended on receiving "Premiums, presents and plunder."[7]

Numerous skirmishes and minor engagements characterize this period of the war on the Niagara. For the local population, trying to survive in the war zone could sometimes result in being host to a spontaneous battle on one's doorstep. For example, on July 8, 1813, a group of local ladies and gentlemen were gathered at the farm of Mr. Peter Ball, near to Four Mile Creek, when polite conversation was interrupted by the sounds of gunfire coming from the adjacent farm, owned by Castle Corus. There, a force of British regulars and Native allies, sent to recover a large chest of medicines and surgical tools hidden during the British retreat in May, had engaged the nearby American picket lines. Witnessing the battle taking place outside their window, the guests watched with alarm as the contest developed and stray shots struck the house. Captain James Kerby, of the Incorporated Militia of Upper Canada, later recorded the course of events:

… among them was Mrs. Law, niece of Mr. Daniel Servos and wife of Captain John Law of the 1st Lincoln Militia.… Captain Law was mortally wounded and his eldest son William Law … killed at the taking of Niagara by the Americans [on] 27 May, 1813. Their youngest son John Law, then a boy of 13, in order to revenge the deaths of his father and brother, got a musket and ammunition and ran down to the front line of the skirmishers, among the Indians and fired some time at the enemy. His mother … fearing … her young son might also be killed, ran down into the very thick of the battle, among the wild and yelling Indians, and inspite of the balls flying all over the field, she found her boy, who was too full of the fright to leave when she called him. When Mrs. Law took hold of him by force and carried him in her arms out of the field to the house, uninjured.[8]

Just over a week later, another engagement took place in the same area that was later described by a participant, Lieutenant T. G. Ridout (3rd York Militia):

On Saturday, 17th, Henry Nelles and I rode down to the Cross Roads, three miles from Niagara, where the Royals, King's, and 600 or 700 Indians are posted. I understood the Americans were advancing into Ball's Fields. Immediately the yell was given and Blackbird and Norton set out with their followers to meet them. Nelles and I rode along, and in a few minutes the skirmish begun by the Western Indians getting upon the left flank and the Five Nations upon the other. The enemy consisted of 500 men. They soon retired, firing heavy volleys upon Blackbird's party, which was the nearest. The road was so straight I could see into town and Nelles and I rode on with the Indians to within one and a quarter miles of Niagara [Newark], when we perceived a large re-inforcement from them, with a piece of artillery, and they advanced … firing grape shot. The Indians scattered into the woods, but we were obliged to keep to the road. By this time, three companies of the Royals, one of militia, and a brass 6-pounder came up and were posted on this side of Ball's field. The Yankees came up and were posted on the other side. We fired for some time, when the Americans thought fit to retreat. At one time, from the farther end of Ball's field a mile and a half this way, the road was covered with Indians, officers, soldiers and horses…. A good many Yankees were killed.[9]

By the end of July, the British cordon around Fort George was drawing ever tighter. Hemmed in on the landward side, the American commander, Brigadier General John Boyd, gained the cooperation of Commodore Chauncey to use of some of his vessels, then anchored off the mouth of the Niagara River for an amphibious assault on Burlington Heights. Laden with troops (200 Infantry, 250 Marines and Seamen), the vessels sailed on July 27th, but due to adverse winds their progress was slowed to a crawl. Fortunately for the British, the American fleet's departure and slow progress was fully observed. In response, Major Titus G. Simons of the Incorporated Militia, serving as the senior militia staff officer at Twelve Mile Creek, was sent an urgent order:

> Dear Major … proceed immediately with your militia to the Head of the Lake, collecting and taking under your command all the regular troops you may find between Shipman's and Burlington

Following his orders, Simons led his own company of the Incorporated Militia, as well as detachments of the York Embodied Militia and 104th Regiment, on a thirty-mile (fifty-kilometer) forced march, as there were not enough wagons to transport the men. Marching through the night, the British/Canadian force arrived at Burlington

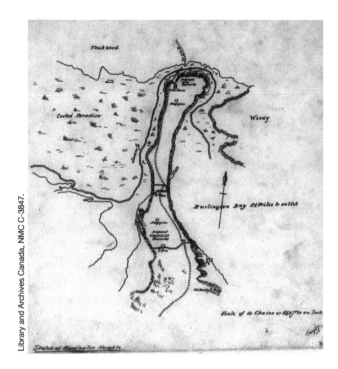

The British supply base of Burlington Heights at Head-of-the-Lake (Hamilton).

Major Titus G. Simons (Incorporated Militia of Upper Canada).

and using your utmost endeavour to forward them whole by wagons if possible. There are strong reasons to apprehend that the enemy means to attack our depot at Burlington , <u>which we must not lose</u>.... It is far too valuable to this army to be lost.[10]

— Lieutenant Colonel Harvey to Major T.G. Simons, July 29, 1813

Library and Archives Canada, NMC C-3847.

Toronto Reference Library, JRR 459.

in time to see the American vessels approaching the low sandbar that divided the end of Lake Ontario from the excellent harbour of Burlington Bay. Taking command of the other units of embodied militia that had turned out from the local area, Simons also witnessed the arrival of Native warriors from the Grand River and two companies of the Glengarry Light Infantry, who had just made a similar forced march along Lake Ontario's north shore from York (Toronto). Together, these units established a strong defensive position across the dominant high ground and awaited the Americans' next move.

Down at the lakefront, after disembarking his forces from the ships and preparing them for a march on the Heights, the American commander, Lieutenant Colonel Winfield Scott, found he was not attacking a surprised supply garrison, but well-prepared enemy formations in commanding defensive positions. Deciding that his force was inadequate to guarantee a military success, Scott hurredly re-embarked his troops aboard their waiting vessels. A bloodless victory had been gained by the Allies, but in his frustration at not being able to destroy Burlington Heights, Scott took his troops north to York, where they landed virtually unopposed, as the garrison of the Glengarry Light Infantry had been taken away for the defence of Burlington and the only militia force (Captain

Jarvie's company of Incorporated Militia) were still on their paroles after their capture by the Americans in April (for details see *The Pendulum of War*). As a result, these militiamen could do nothing to stop the Americans ransacking the military warehouses and destroying property, without running the risk of being accused of breaching their paroles, resulting in arrest and imprisonment, or summary execution.

Upon Scott's return to the Niagara, Boyd — who was anxious to restore the morale of the army in the field and counter the increasingly negative reports of his military inactivity being published in the American press — claimed this expedition as a major military victory. He also began to plan for a further enlarged expedition to capture Burlington Heights with over 1,000 men. However, on the night of August 8/9th, an unusually violent and unexpected thunderstorm swept over Lake Ontario, capsizing Chauncey's warships, *Hamilton* and *Scourge*, and severely damaging several others. In response, the entire fleet abruptly left the area, leaving Boyd to report: "Commodore Chauncey has left this part of the lake and the enemy have now so far the ascendancy as to render the proposed enterprise against his land forces, impracticable…."[11]

During this same period, Brigadier General Porter persuaded several American Native allied bands to return to the fray and cross the Niagara to participate in his raids against private homes and farms between Fort Erie and Chippawa. During these attacks on the civilian population, large quantities of goods and cattle were seized and Porter was inclined to let the Natives retain these spoils, but in this he was overruled by Boyd. Consequently, most of the plundered goods were ordered returned, once again humiliating and frustrating the warriors. By the 14th, General Porter and Major Chapin had brought a combined force of over 500 militia volunteers and Natives to augment the Fort George garrison. On August 17th a sizeable skirmish took place in the woods and fields of the Ball farmstead between an American force of some 300 militia and Natives under Porter, against the British picket and a small force of Native allies under John Norton, numbering less than one hundred in all. Unaware that so many American Native allies were present, Norton and his party, as well as other similar Native detachments, were nearly overrun when they saw what they initially supposed were warriors of their own side retreating in the face of an American militia attack:

> … on first view, I supposed them to have been the detachment of Chippawas … but their appearance soon undeceived me, — I was about to challenge them, when I saw them level to fire, — there were no more than six or seven men near me, — we returned their fire, & retreated on a more advantageous position … there I called upon all that I saw scattered through the field & woods to join, but few obeyed, and we had to take to the woods…. I now thought it improper to persevere any further, seeing the men were rendered unsteady from the uncertainty of receiving any support, & having only thirty or forty of them to oppose a much greater number of the Enemy.[12]

However, when the American supporting regular troops once again deliberately held back and then neglected to consolidate the gains made by their own Native allies, numerous warriors, as well as many from the associated militia, vented their anger by quitting the field and recrossing the Niagara River to the American side. Similarly, this renewed intra-tribal warfare disheartened many British Native allied warriors, causing some to quit the British camp rather than fight against their own tribesmen.

During this summer, weather conditions on the Niagara fluctuated wildly, switching from a short period of extreme heat in early June to four weeks of unseasonable cold and wet weather in late June and early July. This then turned overnight into a period of almost seven weeks of stiflingly high temperatures and drought-like conditions in late July and throughout August. For the British, these conditions were complicated by the fact that their camps and advance positions around Fort George were, of necessity, located according to communication and strategic considerations. Unfortunately, these often coincided with lowland swamps and stagnant water, resulting in a wave of sickness that incapacitated fully a third of the troops in the field.

Nor were things any better inside the tightly restricted American defensive perimeter, as the weather conditions rapidly converted the packed encampment into a fly-infested slum, with heaps of rubbish and refuse accumulating in the tent lines and the stench of overflowing latrines pervading the air. Duty on the outlying pickets was no better, as the men were exposed to the elements for days at a time, in all weathers and under constant threat of attack. Even food stocks were affected, as the weather rapidly increased spoilage of fresh food, while barrels of salted meat were found to have been packed with rotten cuts by unscrupulous suppliers. Even the bread, provided by bakers located just across the river, was found to be mouldy, or so heavily adulterated with

ground plaster of Paris that it could be seen to the naked eye.[13] Inevitably, sickness inside the camp mushroomed from 700 in late July to over 4,500 by the end of August.

With both armies locked in a state of static warfare around Fort George, and the ascendancy of the American flotillas on Lake Ontario and Lake Erie, the British supply lines along these lakes were effectively severed. Thus, both the British "Centre" Division along the Niagara and the "Right" Division on the Detroit frontier found themselves starved of supplies, ammunition, and reinforcements by the normal waterborne routes. Instead, an arduous overland trek had to be made, reducing these badly needed resources to a trickle. Receiving increasingly alarming reports on the state of his forces

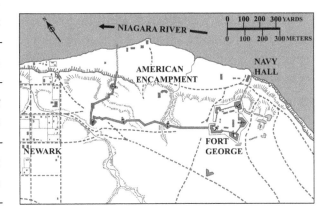

The American fortified encampment at Fort George, Newark (Niagara-on-the-Lake).

in Upper Canada, Sir George Prevost decided to make a personal inspection of the Niagara frontier during the latter part of August:

> On my arrival … I found 2000 British soldiers, on an extended line, cooping up in Fort George, an American force exceeding 4000 men; Feeling desirous of ascertaining in person the enemy's works and of viewing the means he possessed for defending the position, I ordered a general demonstration to be made on Fort George.[14]

On August 24, 1813, Prevost's "demonstration" consisted of two attacking "wings." The "Right" wing consisted of part of the 8th (King's) Regiment (Lieutenant Colonel Battersby) and 49th Regiment (Lieutenant Colonel Plenderleath), who moved from their position at St. Davids in two columns against the four American picket points stationed between the village at the Crossroads (Virgil) and the Niagara River. At the same time, the "Left" wing moved up from its encampment at Four Mile Creek. It too consisted of two columns: the remainder of the 8th (King's) Regiment (Lieutenant Colonel Ogilvie), which advanced along the Niagara Stone Road (modern day Highway 55) and the 104th Regiment (Major Moodie), following the Lakeshore Road. Supporting this advance were the Native warriors and a detachment of newly arrived cavalry from the 19th Light Dragoons (Lieutenant Colonel O'Neil).

Under the cover of a heavy fog, the initial attacks quickly overwhelmed the outlying U.S. pickets and moved on toward the town, where they encountered two columns of American reinforcements moving up from the main American fortifications, using the buildings and fences as cover. The Americans began to contest the British advance, but due to the flanking actions of Major Moodie's column on the far left, the Americans were soon forced to abandon the town and retire into the fort

The Presbyterian Church at Newark (Niagara-on-the-Lake). Because it was used as an observation post by the British on August 24th, it was burnt by the Americans in retaliation.

Toronto Reference Library, JRR 1253.

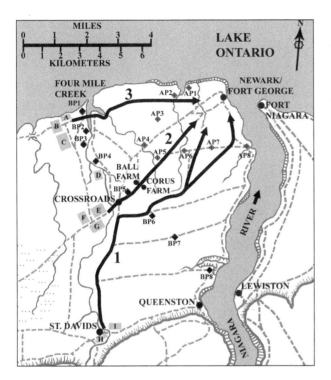

SIR GEORGE PREVOST'S "DEMONSTRATION" AGAINST FORT GEORGE, AUGUST 24, 1813

Key

A, B, C	British military encampments alongside Lake Ontario and the lakeshore road
D	Native allies' encampment
E, F, G	British military encampments at the Crossroads (Virgil)
H, I	British military encampments at St. Davids
BP1 to BP8	British picket positions
AP1 to AP8	American picket positions

1   British "St. Davids" column (1)
2   British "Crossroads" column (2)
3   British "Lakeshore" column (3)

and its adjacent defensive lines. Capturing over fifty Americans and seeing the remainder retreating with speed, Major Moodie believed an opportunity had been created for an immediate assault on the fort. He therefore sought reinforcements to carry through on his advance, while setting up an observation post in the steeple of the Presbyterian church to keep a careful eye on the American movements while the attack was prepared. Instead, he was shocked to learn that the overly cautious Prevost had vetoed any attack and had, instead, ordered a retreat. This was later excused by the general as a stratagem to entice the Americans to leave their defence lines and contest the ground in the open. Naturally the Americans declined to expose themselves and Prevost was reduced to reporting to his superiors in London:

> I found myself close to the camp which is formed on the right of that work [Fort

George], both of them crowded with men, bristled with cannon, and supported by the fire from Fort Niagara.... I am now satisfied that Fort George is not to be reduced, strengthened and supplied as it is by Fort Niagara, without more troops and the co-operation of the fleet and a battery train. To accomplish this object, a double operation becomes necessary, Fort Niagara must be invested, and both places be attacked at the same moment, but my resources and means do not allow me to contemplate so glorious a termination to the campaign in Upper Canada.[15]

— Sir George Prevost to Lord
Bathurst, August 25, 1813

He then returned to Kingston to plan his further actions in Upper Canada.

CHAPTER 3

Going from Bad to Worse:
The Detroit Frontier, July–August 1813

While the British fortunes on the Niagara frontier were improving, the same was not true for General Proctor and his associate senior commander of the British naval forces on Lake Erie, Captain Robert H. Barclay. Both had been forced to contend with the realities of their isolated locations at the end of the British supply line, but now additional factors began to jeopardize their very existence as an effective fighting force.

For Captain Barclay, the American victory at Fort George (see *The Pendulum of War*) had forced the British garrison at Fort Erie to abandon their blockade of the Niagara River. As a result, the Americans had been able to release several sailing vessels previously trapped at the Scajaquada Creek shipyard. After evading Barclay's blockade, these vessels had become part of the growing American flotilla being built and assembled at Presque Isle (Erie) in Pennsylvania, under the command of Master Commandant Oliver H. Perry.

In response, Barclay and Prevost looked to assemble an amphibious strike force that would be transported across Lake Erie aboard Barclay's ships to attack Presque Isle, thus eliminating its growing threat at a stroke. Unfortunately, while this operation was highly time sensitive, and based on the advantage of the moment, the reality was that the state of repair of the British ships and lack of crews made such an operation impossible, unless the fleet was brought into a proper state of readiness in very short order. Consequently, Barclay applied to Sir James Yeo to provide the essential supplies required to put his existing vessels in a seaworthy condition and enable the completion of a powerful

Courtesy of Parks Canada, Fort Malden National Historic Site, FF:77.19.2.

Brigadier General Henry Proctor. A later impression of the general by J.C.H. Forster, circa 1973.

Toronto Reference Library, T 15259.

The senior British naval commander on Lake Erie, Commander Robert H. Barclay.

new warship, the HMS *Detroit*, undergoing construction at Amherstburg. In addition, because his vessels were chronically short of trained naval crews or even experienced civilian sailors, Barclay pressed for manpower to be sent up to crew his flotilla.

Unfortunately, partially as a result of Sir James Yeo's personal bias against his junior commander and Yeo's equal determination to prioritize *his* fleet

on Lake Ontario, Sir James repeatedly ignored Barclay's increasingly desperate and then clamouring pleas, despite supporting documentation from Proctor. In desperation, Barclay went over Yeo's head and appealed directly to Sir George Prevost, who reacted favourably by ordering up fresh supplies and obtaining some 300 seamen from Admiral Warren at Halifax. These he sent into

Upper Canada with the specific intent that they were for the use of Barclay on Lake Erie. Instead, when they arrived at Kingston, Yeo shanghaied the entire lot and assigned them to his command on Lake Ontario. Furthermore, instead of addressing or even partially accommodating Barclay's requests, Yeo's replies became expressions of his personal affront and displeasure at Barclay's letters, as he considered them disrespectful in tone when addressed to himself as Barclay's senior officer.

Margaret Reynolds, artist, circa 1813. Courtesy of Parks Canada, Fort Malden National Historic Site, FF.77.44.1.

The British base at Amherstburg showing the H.M.S. *Detroit* under construction on the slipway, while the H.M.S. *Queen Charlotte* moves upriver under full sail.

Effectively abandoned by his own commander, Barclay resorted to the only thing he could do to fill his list of needs, he turned to Proctor. Despite the cost to his own command in order to oblige, General Prevost assigned some 150 soldiers to man Barclay's vessels. By mid-July, Barclay's preparations were as complete as could be achieved and the small British flotilla set sail to establish what was hoped would be an effective blockade of the American naval base.

During this same period, General Proctor was also in increasing difficulties. Having been consistently starved of reinforcements and supplies under General Sheaffe, he had hoped that General de Rottenburg would release some of the vitally needed troops and supplies previously retained at Burlington Heights and Niagara and transfer them to his thinly stretched command. However, de Rottenburg proved to be even less concerned than Sheaffe with maintaining the British control of the Detroit corridor, especially the occupied territories in Michigan. In fact, without bothering to properly review and consider the importance of Proctor's command to the British war effort, or the difficulties he was under, de Rottenburg also went so far as to inform Proctor that in his opinion the entire Detroit theatre was expendable and therefore would not be reinforced. Revealing his glaring total lack of knowledge on the terrain, geography, and distances involved, de Rottenburg stated that in the event of a major American attack and invasion, the best Proctor could hope to do would be to abandon his Native allies and militias and retreat with his regular troops up Lake Huron to Lake Superior. Following which he could then make an orderly retreat back to Lower Canada by way of the northern interior and Ottawa River, a nice strategy in theory, but in reality a practical impossibility as it meant traversing a distance of at least 800 miles (1,288 kilometers) through some of the wildest and worst terrain to be found in Upper Canada.

Closer to home, Proctor was also bedevilled by a growing list of critical issues that directly threatened his command:

- The Americans were continuing to build their forces at Fort Meigs.
- Bands of enemy marauders were making regular incursions north toward Frenchtown and Detroit, aided and abetted by the local American populace.
- American civilians within the Michigan territory were becoming ever more partisan and active in interfering and blocking British efforts to extend its control across the region.
- His regular forces had been reduced to a skeleton force by battle casualties, sickness, detached duty on the Lake Erie fleet, and an increasing level of desertions.

- In case of an emergency, there was no surety that his embodied militias would turn out or fight in substantial numbers.
- There was no evidence that he was to receive any substantial reinforcements from de Rottenburg by land.
- Despite every effort on their part, Captain Barclay and his Lake Erie flotilla were unable to maintain the essential Lake Erie lifeline of supplies and communications to the Niagara frontier.

Above and beyond this, however, was the growing tension and friction developing between Proctor and the Native allies confederation, headed by Tecumseh. In part, this estrangement had begun following the loss of the promised annual supply of Native presents and supplies at the fall of York in April. To the Native alliance, this loss was one that their white allies should have replaced without delay. However, when replacement gifts were not forthcoming, the Natives' discontent grew. This strain was compounded by the Native's belief that the British were not making sufficient attempts to secure the lands required to create the promised new Native homeland. To top things off, General Proctor had found himself in the embarrassing position of being overwhelmed by the Native response to the earlier British calls for their support. In fact, by the middle of July, the arrival of a succession of flotillas of canoes, crowded with Native warriors (and their extended families) from the Upper Lakes region, had ballooned the Native forces around Amherstburg to over 3,000 warriors, more than six times the entire available British and Canadian force combined. However, while these warriors were keen to take on the Americans, they also looked to Proctor to provide them, and their attendant families, with every conceivable necessity and luxury that was demanded, until the action commenced and booty could be gained. Already pressed to the limit to maintain a steady issue of food for the troops on hand, the addition of these extra mouths, estimated at over 10,000 elders, women, and children, quickly brought the British food supply system at Amherstburg to the brink of exhaustion, leading to the growing spectre of starvation and collapse of command order within a matter of weeks, rather than months.

Proctor recognized that he needed a solution that was logistically feasible, would satisfy his Native allies' demands for a strike against the Americans, and net him some vitally needed supplies into the bargain. Consequently, he proposed making a short-term campaign to seize a number of the American supply bases on the Sandusky River. Unfortunately, this plan did not sit well with the Natives, who wanted the more prominent and readily available target of Fort Meigs as the location for attack.

Despite his severe misgivings on this course of action, the subsequent pressure and implied threats exerted by Tecumseh and his subsidiary chiefs left Proctor with little alternative but to capitulate to the Native demands. In effect, it was now Tecumseh and his warriors who would "call the shots" in how the war on the Detroit frontier would be waged and Proctor was reduced to the junior partner.

Starting out from Amherstburg, the combined force of 3,500 men, made up of some 500 regulars and militia in boats and 3,000 Natives in canoes or marching,[1] reached Fort Meigs on July 21st, thus beginning the second "siege" of that fortification. Warned of the enemy's approach and numbers, the garrison commander, Brigadier General Green Clay, had over 2,000 men under his command, vastly outnumbering Proctor's own troops, but in view of the large enemy Native contingent, Clay chose to remain behind his strengthened walls rather than risk an open battle. Unfortunately for the British cause, as had happened in May (see *The Pendulum of War*), the differing concepts of modes of warfare and battlefield strategies created difficulties and dissention amongst the attackers, leading, on July 25th, to an abortive Native attempt to lure the American garrison out from behind their defences by simulating a battle with a fictitious American relief column being sent by Major General William H. Harrison. When this failed, as General Clay was made aware of the ruse, the increasing frustration expressed by the Native leadership placed Proctor and his men in the dangerous position of either being abandoned by their allies in the face of a superior force of the enemy, or of potentially having some of the more extreme factions of Natives turn on them entirely. Left with little practical alternative, Proctor abandoned the siege and withdrew to his boats on July 30th, whereupon he sought to deflect the Native aggression toward the "real" enemy by proposing the campaign continue against his original target, the American supply bases on the Sandusky River. However, first the small defensive post of Fort Stephenson stood in the way of reaching these bases.

British and Canadian troops aboard Proctor's gunboat flotilla arrived off the Sandusky River on July 31st. These forces advanced upriver toward the fort and, on August 1st, began their preparations to besiege the tiny fortification while awaiting the arrival of the Native contingents, who were marching overland. However, upon their belated arrival, it was found that of the thousands of warriors who had eagerly set out from Amherstburg only three weeks earlier, only a few hundred had made the arduous trek to Fort Stephenson, while the remainder had either headed back to Amherstburg or dispersed entirely.

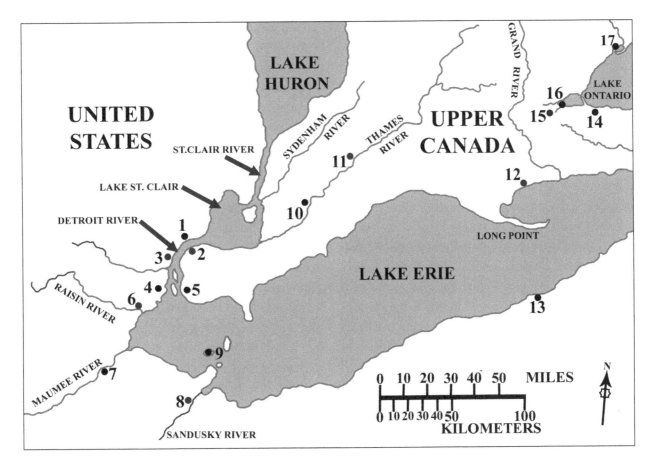

LOCATIONS ALONG THE "DETROIT/WESTERN FRONTIER"

1. Detroit [Fort Detroit]
2. Sandwich (Windsor)
3. Monguagon/Maguaga
4. Browntown
5. Amherstburg [Fort Amherstburg (Fort Malden)]
6. Frenchtown
7. Perrysburg [Fort Meigs]
8. [Fort Stephenson]
9. Put-in-Bay
10. Moravianstown
11. Longwoods
12. Port Dover
13. Presque Isle (Erie, PA)
14. Stoney Creek
15. Ancaster
16. Burlington Heights
17. York (Toronto) [Fort York]

Despite these considerable difficulties, Proctor was still under intense pressure from the Natives to make an attack. After seeing his demand for the fort's surrender rejected, General Proctor began an artillery bombardment late on August 1st with his limited number of artillery pieces. By the following afternoon, although no appreciable visible damage had been done to the fort's defences, the Native's demands for an immediate attack were becoming open threats. Left with little option, Proctor succumbed and three small columns, each consisting of around 150 men, attempted to storm the palisades, backed by detachments of Natives. Coming under fire as they approached, the Natives immediately made a hasty retreat, while the British troops pressed ahead in a determined assault to break through the fort's wooden stockade with axes. However, the equally determined and entrenched garrison of only 160 men, backed by the point-blank fire of a single cannon loaded with a mixture of shot and scrap, were soon able to pin down the attackers in the fort's ditch and inflict heavy casualties on the confined mass of British troops. Inevitably, unable to break into the fort's stockade, the British survivors were either forced back or trapped in the ditch until darkness provided sufficient cover for them to crawl out of range, leaving behind in the process many of their wounded. For Proctor this was the last straw. Ordering the abandonment of the expedition, he set course for Amherstburg, with nothing to show for his efforts but a demoralized military force; a list of twenty-six killed, forty-one wounded, and twenty-nine missing;[2] a frustrated and furious Native contingent; and a greatly diminished stockpile of food and associated supplies.

In one way, Proctor had also just made a lucky escape, as only a few miles down the road, well within striking range and the sound of the battle, General Harrison had assembled a counterattack force of over 2,000 troops and Native allies. This force would have easily overwhelmed the substantially smaller British and Native contingent had it been ordered forward by Harrison, instead of keeping it idle and unused at his encampment.

Upon his return to Amherstburg, Proctor was heartened to find that in his absence some 400 reinforcements had arrived, bringing with them ammunition, entrenching equipment, and food supplies. Although far fewer than was needed to secure the frontier, never mind undertake any offensive operations, these new arrivals were a godsend and hopefully only the precursor of additional support yet to come. Nonetheless, his Native allies continued to be a source of logistical and strategic difficulties. Despite the departure of hundreds of warriors with their attendant families, enough remained to drain Proctor's already dwindling supplies. There was also the potential threat that some, if not all, might switch their allegiances to the Americans. Even Tecumseh was said to be openly voicing his doubts about the alliance in the face of what he saw as a British betrayal of their solemn and long-standing promises.

In the face of these overwhelming situations, Proctor saw no immediate option but to secure his base of operations at Amherstburg and defend his primary responsibility of Upper Canada. Consequently, confidential orders were dispatched to the various garrison posts within the occupied territories in Michigan to strip their local areas of supplies before beginning a disciplined and unannounced retreat on Amherstburg. Inevitably, this news was not long in becoming public, encouraging the more militant Americans to act with greater aggression toward their retreating occupiers. While those less inclined to violence forwarded the welcome news to Harrison, with concurrent demands that he advance immediately with all his forces to secure their properties from further enemy depredations.

Meanwhile, on Lake Erie, Captain Barclay and his conglomerate force were finding the double-duty of maintaining the essential marine supply lines from Fort Erie to Amherstburg, while still maintaining an effective blockade of Presque Isle, increasingly difficult. His vessels were showing signs of requiring critical amounts of repair, while his inexperienced and untrained "land-lubber" crews found themselves overwhelmed by their duties, especially when a series of storms swept over Lake Erie during the latter part of July. As a result, Barclay was repeatedly forced to retire to the shelter of Long Point, leaving the Presque Isle harbour unthreatened. Taking advantage of these absences, Commodore Perry pressed his shipyards into accelerating their building programme and ships crews into preparing themselves to emerge onto the lake to confront their enemy. On July 29th, during one of these British absences, Perry decided that it was a "now or never" moment and, through huge expenditures of effort, the American flotilla was literally manhandled over the harbour's previously protective sandbar into the deeper water of Lake Erie. As a result, when Barclay and his squadron finally reappeared on August 4th it was too late. The Americans were out. In frustration at his own mishandling of the operation, and believing himself to be outmatched in firepower, Barclay and his weatherbeaten ships and crews abandoned the blockade, setting sail for Amherstburg. This departure handed over effective control of Lake Erie to Perry — who took advantage of the opportunity by initiating his own blockade of the British shipborne supply line along Lake Erie's north shore. Proctor and Barclay were not only effectively, but physically, cut off and isolated.

CHAPTER 4

Move and Counter Move:
August–September 1813

Having failed to conquer the Niagara frontier, and with the Detroit frontier still in a state of flux, the American administration decided to target the St. Lawrence River corridor and Lower Canada, aiming to sever the British supply line into Upper Canada. Convening a council of war at Sackets Harbor on August 26, 1813, General Wilkinson and his staff discussed several alternative strategies before deciding:

> ... to rendezvous the whole of the troops on the lake in this vicinity, and in cooperation with the squadron, make a bold feint at Kingston, slip down the St. Lawrence, lock up the enemy in our rear, to starve and surrender, or oblige him to follow us without artillery, baggage, or provisions, and eventually to lay down his arms; to sweep the St. Lawrence of armed vessels and in concert with the division under Major General Hampton, to take possession of Montreal.[1]

To personally oversee the planning for this campaign, Secretary of War Armstrong and a substantial staff relocated to Sackets Harbor in early September, while General Wilkinson travelled to Fort George with a sizeable part of Chauncey's fleet to transport the required troops back to Sackets Harbor. Once there, however, General Wilkinson was incapacitated by what he referred to as "a severe and unremitting malady ... with much depression of the head and stomach."[2] Finally, on September

16th he "escaped from [his] pallet with a giddy head and trembling hand."[3]

Pressed by the local Native leaders to recover the initiative on the Niagara frontier, Wilkinson reluctantly agreed to make a probe of the British positions. However, his troops only made a half-hearted advance resulting in the burning of some civilian homes and a small military barrack near the Twelve Mile Creek, before they abandoned any further offensive action and returned to Fort George. Wilkinson issued orders for the withdrawal of most of the regular troops from the Niagara and their replacement with assorted detachments of militia.

Unfortunately, because the fleet of longboats and scows used in May had remained beached throughout the summer they had become totally unseaworthy. Further valuable time was therefore lost undertaking repairs. Seeking to salvage something from the unsatisfactory situation on the Niagara, Wilkinson wrote to Armstrong proposing a breakout attempt from Fort George, backed by the guns of Chauncey's ships. However, the unexpected appearance of Yeo's fleet and its subsequent manoeuvres (aimed at drawing Chauncey's flotilla into a close-range action) further stalled any land-based offensive for two weeks, whereupon an answer arrived from Armstrong, expressly vetoing Wilkinson's proposal. After further difficulties

and delays, the first wave of boats, loaded with over 1,500 troops, sailed for Sackets Harbor on September 25th, but within hours they were driven back when bad weather moved in, making safe passage impossible. Two days later another attempt was made, only to be immediately recalled, as Yeo's ships had again appeared on the horizon.

Under pressure to clear the way for Wilkinson's forces to leave, Chauncey's flotilla sailed to engage the British off the mouth of the Niagara River. Following considerable manoeuvring, the two opposing fleets finally began firing. Onshore, men from the two armies mutually suspended their own hostilities and eagerly cheered on their respective sides as the conflict developed. After about two hours, with serious damage done to vessels on both sides, the British squadron appeared to have come off worst, as it broke off from the action and retired up the lake toward Burlington, followed closely by the Americans. Anchoring under the protection of the lee of the land, the British vessels stood on the defensive until the Americans finally withdrew to the Niagara River, making claims of a decisive victory. However, as a result of the action the American vessels had to undergo significant repairs before they could escort Wilkinson's convoy to Sackets Harbor, leaving the general complaining that he "had difficulties, perplexities and anxieties sufficient to discompose a saint."[4]

Under stormy skies, the American regular forces finally set sail on October 1st, followed a day later by their commander. Wilkinson left a small force of regulars, artillery, and militia at Fort George, under the command of a frustrated Colonel Winfield Scott, who dearly wanted to participate in the forthcoming offensive instead of being left behind.

Receiving reports of the American redeployment, General de Rottenburg took the gamble of reducing his forces on the Niagara by taking the 49th, 104th, and Voltigeur regiments back to Kingston as a counter to the American build-up at Sackets Harbor. He also called upon Prevost to recognize that the defence of Upper Canada could not be maintained if the proper resources were not applied to the duty.

> What with sickness and desertion … my situation becomes dayly more desperate. More than a thousand men are laid up and officers in a still greater proportion. There is no thoroughly healthy spot to retire to as far as York. Burlington is quite as bad as here. The fever and ague rages and the inhabitants are as sickly as the soldiers. If you cannot send me fresh troops, the country will be lost for the want of hands to defend it…. If I am attacked and forced back, one-half of the sick will be lost for want of conveyance.[5]
>
> — General de Rottenburg to
> Sir George Prevost, September 17, 1813

Unfortunately, to the Upper Canada populace and the Native allies in particular, this British redeployment appeared to be an abandonment of General Vincent and a precursor to a withdrawal from Upper Canada entirely, especially in the light of subsequent events on the Detroit frontier.

CHAPTER 5

The Vice Begins to Tighten:
The Detroit Frontier, September 1813

As summer turned to autumn on the Detroit frontier, General Proctor and Captain Barclay were both running out of options. For Captain Barclay, the loss of control on Lake Erie in August had cut off his lifeline of heavy armament and ship's fittings. He also learned that Perry was acting in concert with General Harrison at the Sandusky River to prepare an invasion fleet of landing craft for use by his army.

Denied any new supplies, Barclay again used his own resources and ingenuity to ready his flotilla for action. He ordered every spare part stripped from his existing vessels, and even cannibalized less seaworthy ones to complete the fitting-out of the *Detroit.* The only reinforcements he had received in the previous month were a footsore party of forty-one seamen, who arrived overland on September 2nd. He therefore applied to General Proctor again for a new round of assistance. In response, despite suffering his own critical shortages, Proctor not only transferred 250 men to Barclay's command, but approved the stripping of Fort Amherstburg's ramparts and magazines to supply the essential heavy-calibre "broadside" artillery pieces and ammunition needed aboard Barclay's ships.

Similarly, General Proctor, while gratified that the recent arrival of small detachments of troops had brought his fighting force to around 1,130 men of all ranks, making it the largest since the beginning of the war, he had also run out of options for effectively maintaining his command. His coffers were empty, preventing the purchase of supplies, and his existing food stocks were counted to last only a matter of days, thanks primarily to the ongoing demands of the still huge contingent of Native hangers-on. In fact, the starving Natives were unable to survive on the reduced rations issued by the British and had been pressed to the desperate necessity of rustling oxen, milk cows, sheep, and even dogs, to fill their empty bellies. Matters came to a head when a local businessman, Thomas Verchères de Boucherville, succeeded in bringing a small convoy of supplies aboard a number of canoes into Amherstburg. Having made a shore-hugging journey down Lake Erie, these goods were put on sale at extortionate and inflated prices. Nonetheless, pandemonium ensued as virtually the entire local civilian population, military staff, officers and men, not to mention Natives bearing military-issued scrip (money bills), descended on Boucherville's store. Within hours the shelves were stripped bare, allowing Boucherville to later boast:

> I was so busy in the store that I scarcely had an opportunity to examine my invoices and place the goods on the shelves…. By this time, they were in need of everything and no one wanted to miss a splendid chance…. The first day, I took in more than two thousand, four hundred dollars…. I was master of the situation….[1]

Faced with a near riot and his options at an end, Proctor consulted with Barclay. As the *Detroit* had finally been launched and fitted out, they both agreed that with no sign of further reinforcements arriving by the overland route, the British supply route on Lake Erie cut, and Harrison and Perry on the verge of making a major invasion from across the lake, their only recourse was to take the desperate gamble that Barclay and his assortment of mis-armed and motley-crewed vessels could pull off a miracle and not only open the lines of communication, but also make a knockout blow against the American fleet, now reported as anchoring at Put-in-Bay.[*2]

On the afternoon of September 9th, the British flotilla, such as it was,[*3] sailed to seek out and engage the Americans. The situation was desperate, but not devoid of hope, as Captain Barclay later recounted in a report to Yeo.

> I [was] obliged to sail with the squadron, deplorably manned as it was, to enable us to get stores and provisions of every description…. So perfectly destitute of provisions was the post, that there was not a day's flour left in the store and the crews of the squadron were on half-allowances of many things and when that was done, there was no more. Such were

the motives that induced Major General to concur in the necessity of a battle being risqued…. No intelligence of seamen having arrived, I sailed….[4]

Shortly before noon on the following day, the sounds of distant thunder could be heard reverberating from the south on Lake Erie, and clouds of grey-white smoke dotted the horizon, though the sky was clear. These echoes of the battle that was obviously being fought continued for nearly three hours, following which silence fell once more and the clouds dissipated. However, during the remainder of that day and the next, no vessel or courier ship arrived to report on the result of what was surely a major action. By September 12th, Proctor finally had to accept the inevitable, that some catastrophe had occurred. In fact, following a hard and close-fought battle between the two fleets, that inflicted casualties ranging from 30 percent aboard the British *Detroit* and *Queen Charlotte*, to 60 percent aboard the American *Lawrence*, the entire British squadron had been beaten into submission and forced to surrender to the Americans, leaving no one to bring the disastrous news back to General Proctor.

Proctor was now faced with the reality that his tenuous hold on the Detroit frontier had been entirely wiped out. His marine supply line to his base of supplies and reinforcements was irrevocably and

BATTLE OF LAKE ERIE, SEPTEMBER 10, 1813

American Vessels[2]

Lawrence (O.H. Perry)
Niagara (Jesse Elliott)
Caledonia (Daniel Turner)
Ariel (John Packet)
Somers (Thomas Almy)
Scorpion (Stephen Champlin)
Porcupine (George Senat)
Tigress (Augustus Conklin)
Trippe (Thomas Holdup)

British Vessels[3]

Detroit (Robert Barclay)
Queen Charlotte (Robert Finnis)
Lady Prevost (Edward Buchan)
General Hunter (George Bignell)
Little Belt (Commander Unknown)
Chippewa (John Campbell)

N.B the British flotilla's crews consisted of an estimate of:

250 all ranks from the 41st Regiment (Lieutenant Arthur O'Keefe) and Royal Newfoundland Fencible Regiment (Lieutenant James Garden)
53 sailors (all ranks)
135 Colonial Marine sailors and Voyageurs
2 Native allied volunteers

Courtesy of the Buffalo and Erie County Historical Society Research Library, Buffalo, NY.

The Battle of Lake Erie, the action that began the series of military catastrophes that lost the British control of Western Upper Canada for the remainder of the war.

completely severed. The greater bulk of his artillery was lost aboard the fleet, and he had lost almost 30 percent of his effective fighting force, all without him firing a shot. Faced with these circumstances, the only feasible response was for him to order a general evacuation, retreat from his exposed positions along the Detroit frontier, and attempt to link up with Vincent's forces beyond the Grand River. Logical and necessary as this might have been, Proctor knew he would have to overcome the opposition of his Native allies, who would vehemently object to any retreat as an abandonment of the British treaties of mutual support that the Natives had trusted and relied upon when they answered the call to fight on the side of the British in 1812.

The following day (September 13th), Proctor declared martial law in order to requisition all available horses and wagons, as well as whatever foodstuffs and other supplies could be brought in to sustain his troops on the march. Already suspicious about the lack of official news following the distinct sounds of heavy cannon fire on the lake on the 10th and the declaration of martial law, the subsequent appearance of requisition parties triggered an immediate panic in the civilian populace and the expected negative backlash within the Native encampments. Forced to address these issues, Proctor made no attempt to stop the civilians from gathering their possessions and beginning the long trek east, as the absence of every person reduced his burden of protecting and feeding these individuals. The Natives, however, were another matter. From long and sometimes bitter experience, Proctor knew the tribal leaders would require delicate handling if they were to be persuaded to maintain their allegiance to the Crown and voluntarily abandon their lands and immediate hopes of gaining a homeland. Calling together an assembly of the Native leadership on September 15th, he presented his case for retreat and, as expected, triggered an immediate backlash of objection and anger amongst most of the tribal elders, especially Tecumseh, who made a vociferous condemnation of Proctor personally and the British as a whole for breaking faith. Such was the degree of animosity expressed that the British were told they might find themselves prevented

or attacked by their erstwhile allies if they began a unilateral retreat. Under these conditions, the assembly broke up in disorder.

Over the next two days, Proctor made strenuous efforts to placate Tecumseh and his more vehement cohorts, only to fail on every count. In the end, and only after holding a private meeting with Tecumseh, Proctor was able to gain a tenuous and reluctant assent by the majority of chiefs to undertake a "partial" retreat as far as the "Forks" on the Thames River (Chatham). In return, Proctor made assurances that *once there* defences would be established, and that if the Americans did invade and follow they would be brought to battle and defeated. Unfortunately, Proctor's interpreter, Matthew Elliott (British Indian Department), expressed Proctor's assurances in terms that led the Natives to believe that *by the time* they arrived at the Thames, defences would *already* be erected and defended. This miscommunication, whether deliberate or accidental, laid the foundation for the disasters that were to follow.

With the greater mass of civilians already on the road, and under the suspicious and baleful eyes of his Native contingent, Proctor began his retreat on September 22nd when his main baggage wagons, accompanied by a strong contingent of guards to prevent looting, were sent off, well ahead of the main column. A small flotilla of the remaining gunboats and bateaux sailed away with supplies and ammunition, on top of which were distributed the sick, the wounded, and all remaining military dependents, made up of the regiment's women and children. The following day, Proctor and his main column, shadowed by a veritable cloud of refugees and Natives, marched out from Amherstburg as the shipyard and fortifications were set alight in an attempt to deny the Americans any cover or item that might prove useful.

CHAPTER 6

The Vice Closes

On the other side of Lake Erie, following Perry's victory nothing stood in the way of Major General William H. Harrison's planned invasion. Had he chosen to he could have marched his entire army around the head of Lake Erie and crossed directly at the mouth of the Detroit River. Instead, while a significant force was dispatched to secure that flank, the bulk of his army rendezvoused with Perry's ships for transportation to the Canadian shore. Harrison's forces were initially composed of some 8,000 troops, drawn from detachments of regular regiments and the Kentucky, Ohio, and Pennsylvania militias. However, after deducting the men marching toward Detroit, the remainder was further reduced by a number of militia units exercising their constitutional rights not to fight outside of the territory of the United States. For the

Courtesy of the Buffalo and Erie County Historical Society Research Library, Buffalo, NY.

Major General William H. Harrison (governor, Indiana Territory).

rest, the prospect of booty, glory, and, in some cases, revenge (principally on the Natives) was sufficient cause for ignoring the letter of the law to join Harrison's invasion.

The invasion force of fourteen vessels and over one hundred boats and bateaux[1] initially sailed to Put-in Bay on September 22nd, to make final preparations to land in hostile territory while under fire. Instead, reconnaissance vessels returned the following day with the welcome news that Amherstburg appeared abandoned and its fortifications reduced to smouldering ash.

Following a delay caused by bad weather, on September 26, 1813, the initial wave of American troops landed unopposed at Bar Point, a few miles below Amherstburg, followed shortly thereafter by the bulk of Harrison's invading army, composed of some 2,000 regulars and over 3,000 Kentucky and Pennsylvania militia.[2]

At the same time, General Proctor was at Sandwich (Windsor) in the

Right: Locations along the Detroit River.

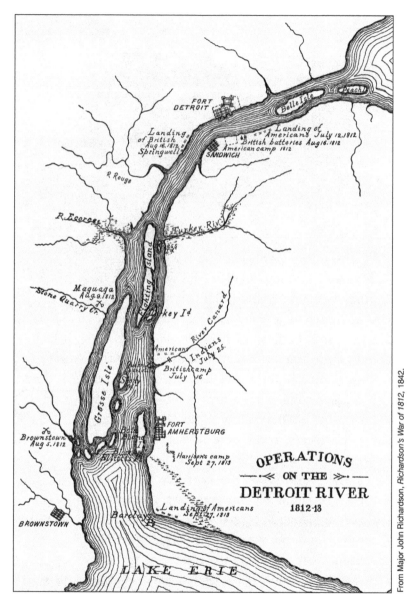

From Major John Richardson, *Richardson's War of 1812*, 1842.

final stages of withdrawing his last forces from the west bank of the Detroit River. He had also hoped to include a large contingent of Native warriors from the tribes on the far side of the river. However, in this he was disappointed, as they almost unanimously refused to obey his directives and openly repudiated their allegiance to the British cause. Left with no recourse but to abandon his position in the face of the arrival of news that Harrison had finally landed and was in occupation of Amherstburg, Proctor began the next stage of his retreat, along the south shore of Lake St. Clair toward the mouth of the Thames River.

In the days that followed, the sequence of events that occurred followed an increasingly depressing pattern for Proctor's force:

— September 28th: Proctor's main column and accompanying boat flotilla moved up Lake St. Clair toward the mouth of the Thames River, while Tecumseh and a strong force of Native warriors remained at Sandwich, hoping to attack the advance of the American invaders, but without result.

— September 29th: The British main column passed the mouth of the Thames and encamped, while the boat flotilla was passed over the river-mouth delta sandbars, but only by dint of heavy labour and the partial unloading and then reloading of each vessel in turn. At this point, Proctor still anticipated that no significant pursuit would be made by Harrison once he regained control of the Detroit frontier. At Sandwich, Tecumseh's Native force marched to rejoin Proctor, but lost numerous warriors through desertion. That night, news arrived of the American occupation of Sandwich.

— September 30th: Against his own better judgement and the advice of his officers, Proctor kept the bulk of his force at the mouth of the Thames — probably to placate Tecumseh and the other Native chiefs. However, he did order the pushing on of his supply boats, all unnecessary wagons and encumbrances, civilian refugees, and Native families, upriver toward the Forks. Native warrior desertions escalated, resulting in the parallel departure of entire Native families and increased reports of missing supplies and equipment.

— October 1st: Due to Native stragglers, Proctor was again forced to retain part of his force at the mouth of the Thames and prevented from destroying the bridges marking his line of retreat (as it would strand those not already passed and thereby alienate and aggravate his increasingly insubordinate Native allies). In addition, bad weather and torrential freezing rains turned the already heavily overburdened and over-travelled roadway into a mud-caked quagmire, slowing the retreat even further. To speed things up, Proctor made a personal inspection upriver to assess the conditions along the line of retreat, but in his absence news arrived at the British rearguard that the Americans had pushed gunboats and troopships into Lake St. Clair. This represented a significant threat to the rearguard whereby enemy forces could be landed on the lakeshore to cut off their line of retreat. Consequently, Proctor's second-in-command, Colonel Augustus Warburton, ordered the retreat recommence immediately, but still did not order the destruction of any of the bridges once the last of the British troops had passed through. By nightfall, the main part of the British column had encamped at the small hamlet at Dolsen's, some eight miles (12.8 kilometers) upriver, with the British troops occupying the north bank and the Natives the south. Here it was expected that a defensive position would be constructed around the already established cluster of workshops, residences, and associated outbuildings. Camp ovens were erected and immediately began the production of bread to feed the near starving troops, not to mention the civilians and hordes of Natives that had also halted their passage and now were encumbering both the retreat and the establishment of a defensive perimeter.

THE ROUTES TAKEN BY THE OPPOSING ARMIES IN THE RETREAT FROM SANDWICH (WINDSOR) TO THE BATTLEFIELD NEAR MORAVIANSTOWN IN SEPTEMBER–OCTOBER 1813

1. September 28th–29th: The leading elements of the British land forces and the convoy of accompanying boats (1) enter the Thames River Valley from Lake St. Clair. September 29th: The rearguard of the British forces reach Louis Trudelle's farm (1a) and remain there till October 1st. American forces (1b) arrive at the mouth of the River Thames on October 2nd.

2. October 1st–2nd: British forces cross the Thames River at Dolsen's (2) and begin to prepare defences, while part of the Native allies continue upriver to the Forks of the Thames. The British hurriedly evacuate the position on October 3rd (noon). October 3rd (p.m.) American forces reach and encamp at Drake's farm (2a) on the south side of the Thames River, just downriver from Dolsen's, which they also overrun and occupy. The American advance continues along the south bank on the 4th (2b).

3. October 3rd (p.m.): British forces retreat to the "Forks of the Thames" (Chatham) (3) and encamp on both sides of the river. October 4th (a.m.) while the British forces continue to retreat, the British Native allies (3a) make a rearguard stand against the Americans at the Forks, along the McGregor Creek.

4. October 4th (p.m.): American forces reach Traxler's farm (4) and encamp. They also witness the burning of British supply gunboats in the river at Bowle's farm (4a), just upriver. British forces reach Cornwall's Mill/ Sherman's farm/Richardson's farm (4b) and encamp, setting up supply kitchens. The Native allies encamp at Arnold's Mills (5).

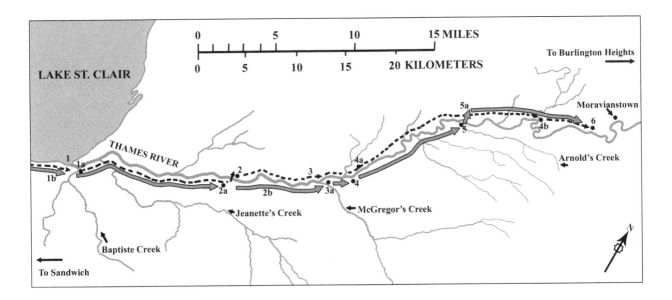

5. October 5th (a.m.): American forces reach Arnold's Mill (5) and capture Proctor's ammunition boats. They then cross to the north bank of the Thames River (5a) and advance to Cornwall's Mill/Sherman's farm/Richardson's farm (4b), overrunning the previously abandoned British encampment and taking the partially prepared British rations. They then advance on Moravianstown to attack the British.

6. The battleground for the Battle of the Thames/Moravianstown.

— October 2nd: With no American pursuit appearing, Proctor believed the immediate threat had passed, allowing him time to prepare his defensive positions on the riverbanks. Unfortunately, a report by his engineering officer, Captain Dixon, indicated that the Dolsen's position was devoid of natural defensive advantages, while the proposed secondary position at the Forks, four miles (6.5 kilometers) upstream, while defensively suitable, was devoid of shelter to accommodate the exhausted troops from the increasingly cold and wet weather. As a result, the only remaining point at which a defensive stand could be made, that also provided shelter, was further upriver at the small community of Moravianstown (Fairfield), an arduous 26 miles (42 kilometers) away.

— October 3rd: General Proctor decided that the continued absence of an American pursuit allowed him time to make a personal reconnaissance of Moravianstown. In his absence, he left orders for the destruction of the bridges downriver and the establishment of earthwork fortifications at Dolsen's. Little was accomplished, however, as the previously accessible entrenching tools had been inadvertently re-stowed at the bottom of one of the accompanying supply vessels when they had previously crossed the rivermouth sandbar. By noon, reports arrived of extensive American troop movements downriver and the capture of the detachment sent to destroy the bridges. In response, Colonel Warburton ordered an immediate retreat by his troops, forcing them to abandon their ovens. However, he again issued no associated orders for the Natives, the accompanying vessels in the river, or the evacuation of a large party of military families travelling in those vessels — leaving them all to make their own way upriver toward the Forks of the Thames. Meanwhile, unaware of developments downriver, Proctor had made his inspection at Moravianstown and concluded that it was a suitable defensive position. He also

decided to remain for the night before returning to join his troops.

During this same period, Harrison's army, unencumbered and aggressively champing at the bit to catch and thrash their long time enemies, had been moving swiftly in pursuit.

— September 28th: American advance forces reached the Canard River and crossed unopposed.
— September 29th: The main column occupied Sandwich (Windsor), while on the river seventeen

Right: Although some of these images were painted twenty or more years after the war, they still indicate the primitive "frontier" conditions that remained at that time and challenged the movement of troops in Upper Canada during the war of 1812–1815.

(1) *Between York and Cobourg*, J.P. Cockburn, artist, circa 1830.

(2) *Making a Road*, J.P. Cockburn, artist, circa 1830.

(3) *Making a Clearing*, G. Whitmore, circa 1836.

(4) *A First Settlement*, W.H. Bartlett, circa 1842.

(5) *Corduroy Road near Guelph, Upper Canada*, H.B. Martin, artist, circa 1832. A "corduroy" road, constructed of baulks of cut timber, was designed to create a raised pathway for wagons to drive (bone-jarringly) through regions of wet or swampy ground.

Library and Archives Canada, C-12613.

Library and Archives Canada, C-12630.

Library and Archives Canada, C-040316.

Library and Archives Canada, C-041662.

Library and Archives Canada, C-115040.

U.S. naval vessels and gunboats, accompanied by over 150 supply craft and bateaux, also arrived.[3] Harrison officially decreed the long-awaited American re-occupation of the Michigan territory, but retained Proctor's previous edicts on the imposition of martial law.

— September 30th: While the bulk of the American pursuit force (estimated at 3,500 all ranks),[4] marched from Sandwich toward the Thames River, Harrison's distrust of the large number of former British allied Natives remaining on the Detroit frontier forced him to leave behind a strong garrison at Detroit. By nightfall, some of Perry's gunboats had forced their way through the St. Clair River rapids into Lake St. Clair.

— October 1st: The American advance rapidly gained ground on the British, due to a lack of encumbrances and the failure of the British to destroy the bridges over the intervening creeks.

— October 2nd: The American vessels *Scorpion*, *Porcupine*, and *Tigress*, under Perry's direct command, entered the mouth of the Thames River, accompanied by over fifty smaller gunboats and bateaux.

— October 3rd: The American advance guard overtook and captured part of the British rearguard while in the act of destroying the bridge crossing Jeanette's Creek. By nightfall, American troops had reached Drake's farmstead, across from the Dolsen farm and occupied the abandoned British encampment.

CHAPTER 7

A Crushing Defeat

On the morning of October 4th, at Moravianstown, when General Proctor heard that the Americans were closing on his rearguard, he immediately began the twenty-mile (32 kilometers) journey to rejoin his forces. Meanwhile, at the Forks, Colonel Warburton was faced with an increasingly irate Tecumseh and his Native followers. For, following the previous day's precipitant retreat, where half of the remaining Native warrior contingent had deserted, those who had remained had come close to violence when they arrived at the Forks to find that instead of entering a series of prepared defences, ready and waiting for use, there was nothing to indicate that the British would be making a stand. Leaving them, and especially Tecumseh, believing that they had been deliberately betrayed and were about to be abandoned in the face of their mortal enemy.

This impression was not entirely mistaken, for although the issue of miscommunication could be laid at the feet of the British Indian Department's translator, Matthew Elliot, the fact was that by this time, many of the British officers had become highly critical of Proctor for allowing the Natives to dictate the pace of the army's retreat. While a small but vocal cadre voiced the opinion that it was time to cut their losses and unilaterally pull out — abandoning the Natives and whatever could not be transported, in the interest of preserving the core military force for future use.

Facing the difficult decision of either making a stand, as the Natives demanded, or continuing the withdrawal toward Proctor at Moravianstown, Warburton was relieved of this decision when news simultaneously arrived that Proctor had arrived and ordered that the retreat continue and that the Natives were not only in accord about making a further withdrawal but were willing to act as a rearguard and make a stand to delay the American advance.

Retreating his column a distance of a further four miles (6.5 kilometers) Warburton met Proctor at the Bowles' farm, the highest practical point for the navigation of the larger boats accompanying the retreat. As these larger vessels could no longer be navigated further upriver, Proctor ordered that as much as possible be transferred to the already overloaded smaller bateaux. Any remaining supplies were then to be burned, while the boats, *Mary*, *Miamis*, and *Ellen*, were to be set on fire and scuttled.

The retreat, which had previously been accomplished with some degree of order, was on the verge of disintegrating into a rout. The Native contingent was evaporating by the hour, the civilian and militia refugees who were already upriver were bordering on panic, clogging the road in their attempts to escape, while those who had already fallen behind were being overtaken and captured/looted by the American advance forces. Proctor's regular troops had hardly eaten since they had lost their ovens at Dolsen's and were angered that instead of being given the chance to grab what might have remained in the boats, it was now being destroyed before their eyes as they were marched off.

Back at the Forks, the Americans reached the river junction only to find the bridges destroyed and the point apparently defended. The defending force consisted only of Tecumseh's warriors, but because Harrison believed there also had to be a hidden British regular component, he delayed attacking until his artillery could be brought up. Once Harrison's guns opened the action, it quickly became evident that no British force was replying and the Natives had abandoned their positions. After repairing the bridges, Harrison's men pressed forward with an increasing degree of confidence and enthusiasm as the signs of a British rout multiplied. Having already overtaken an increasing number of military stragglers and groups of civilians, as well as a steady stream of abandoned goods and impedimenta, they now came across wholesale lots of equipment and supplies, some burned and unusable but some intact and there for the taking. There was also the impressive sight of three British gunboat/supply boats burning fiercely in the river, their ammunition cargoes detonating, sending debris flying in all directions. Finally, and most satisfying, they came across two 24-pounder cannon, abandoned in the mud, which proved to be pieces taken by General Brock at the surrender of Detroit, just over a year previous.

The stage was set for the final showdown.

THE BATTLE OF THE THAMES (MORAVIANSTOWN), OCTOBER 5, 1813

As the encumbered British force prepared to make its final slow march toward Moravianstown, the Americans moved first, advancing rapidly along the riverbank road. As a result, with Proctor once again absent from his corps (he was at Moravianstown, making preparations for his army's imminent arrival), the American approach triggered yet another hurried order from Colonel Warburton to retreat. For the second time in a few days, the troops, who were in the process of preparing what little food they had left for their main meal, were forced to abandon their half-prepared food and march away hungry. Reaching a point a little below (west of) Moravianstown, news from the rear indicated that the Americans were rapidly closing on the rearguard, stationed only a mile (1.6 kilometers) downriver. Without the apparent time to reach Moravianstown and establish a proper line of defence, and the subsequent hurried arrival of General Proctor, the troops received orders to halt where they stood and deploy into line-of-battle.

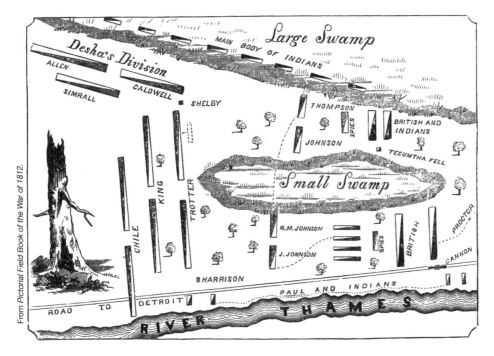

From *Pictorial Field Book of the War of 1812.*

The Battle of the Thames (Moravianstown).

65

Curiously, from the remaining small park of artillery that was available, only one piece, a 6-pounder, was ordered to unlimber and join the line. In addition, thanks to Warburton's repeated failure to order the simultaneous movement of the boats in the river during the latest evacuation, these vessels had been allowed to lag behind the main body of troops, a dangerous situation that Warburton had failed to address. Proctor, shocked by Warburton's glaring error, ordered their immediate retrieval as they contained the *entire* supply of reserve ammunition for the army! To this end, he sent a party of mounted dragoons to expedite the order. Instead, they returned with the disastrous news that not only had the boats and their crews been overrun and captured, but that the army's field ammunition reserve, being transported in a number of wagons, had also been left behind during the morning's hasty retreat and had likewise fallen into enemy hands.

Proctor was now left with the singular problem of being expected to conduct a battle where:

- He had no accurate intelligence detailing the enemy's strength, composition, or dispositions.
- His Native allies were apparently on the verge of routing or rebelling.
- Many of his own troops were detached on guard and transport duties and therefore unavailable for immediate use. Others had already been captured, being part of the ammunition boat and wagon crews now lost to the enemy
- Those troops that were at hand were exhausted, dispirited, and hungry, with no hope of reinforcement or support, and with only as much ammunition as each man was carrying in his cartridge box, which for many amounted to less than sixty rounds apiece — only enough to conduct a steady fight for about an hour, if he was lucky!

Unfortunately for historians, due to the chaos of the moment and the loss of many official British records after the battle, the exact number and composition of those troops positioned on the field is not accurately documented. It was likely composed principally of the remnants of the 41st Regiment, broken down according to a subsequent regimental roll to: 4 staff, 19 officers, 4 drummers, and 341 other ranks. This was supplemented by small detachments drawn from the Royal Newfoundland Regiment, the 10th Royal Veterans Regiment, the Royal Artillery, Royal Artillery Drivers, and Provincial Cavalry, amounting to less than 500 men of all ranks.[1]

Despite his own paucity of numbers in relation to the estimated over 3,000 in the enemy's force, Proctor used the available terrain to its best advantage, deploying his troops across a narrow parcel of

From Pictorial Field Book of the War of 1812.

The battlefield near Moravianstown in the post-war period.

open ground, where his left flank was secured by the river and his right by a heavily wooded swamp, thus forcing the enemy to make any attack through a restricted channel and directly to his front. As well as being broken by a number of outcrops of low vegetation, bushes, and trees, the centre of the field was obstructed by an area of low boggy ground that hopefully would be a major impediment to any mounted troops the enemy sought to use. Within the margins of the main swamp on his right, some 400–600 Natives,[2] under a still determined and dynamic Tecumseh, took up positions forward of the British line and amongst the fallen trees and heavy undergrowth. From there they could not only protect themselves but also throw their firepower on the enemy's flank if it tried to advance on the British line. On his left, Proctor positioned

his lone artillery piece, a 6-pounder, supported by a small detachment of infantry and Provincial Light Dragoons. Across the centre the infantry companies stood in their normal shoulder-to-shoulder formation, necessary to deliver the standard infantry volleys that characterized the fighting of a battle with single-shot, muzzle-loading muskets.

Having completed this deployment, Proctor appeared to have second thoughts. This may have been due to demands made by Tecumseh, or perhaps his own reconsideration of his vulnerability in a single line. Regardless of the reason, and with the enemy supposedly almost in sight, Proctor dropped a bombshell by ordering a complete repositioning of his forces.

Withdrawing two of his strongest companies (the Grenadier and 1st Centre) from the line, he posted them at a distance of an estimated hundred yards (91.5 meters) behind his now disrupted and broken front. To fill the resultant intercompany gaps, Proctor could have simply repositioned each of the remaining companies, leaving slightly larger intervals of space between the solid blocks of men. Or he could have redeployed the two ranks into a single extended rank, but still shoulder-to-shoulder. Instead, Proctor ordered each company to remain in two ranks, but with the front and rear ranks spaced further apart and each man distinctly separated from his right- and left-hand fellow by a couple of paces. This formation was one that had been used in heavily wooded conditions during the American Revolutionary War, more than thirty years previous, but his currrent body of troops were probably neither familiar with, nor trained to adopt it as part of their standard fighting manoeuvres. Why he chose this disposition is unexplainable, as the ground was relatively open and consequently stripped the men of the "centre" companies of their trained discipline of fighting as a solid coherent unit, while denying those of the "flank" companies of their additional training to act in an open and mobile formation. Nonetheless, this was the formation adopted by the British as they stood idle, instead of preparing any fieldworks, and waited for over two hours for the Americans to appear from the opening in the riverbank trail.

Downriver, General Harrison had been equally occupied in preparing his army for what appeared to be an imminent clash with Proctor. Using his mounted troops in the vanguard, Harrison had made several captures that morning, including two gunboats and the bateaux containing Proctor's ammunition, entrenching tools, and provisions, not to mention their crews, a host of stragglers, and several military families. Having travelled along the south side of the Thames, Harrison's army forded the cold river and continued the pursuit along the north bank, thankfully warming themselves for a passing moment at the abandoned British camp-fires and grabbing any food they found to eat upon the march. The next coup came in the form of overtaking Proctor's ammunition wagons, mired in the heavily cut-up trackway that passed for the main highway in this part of the country.

General Harrison also elicited valuable intelligence from his prisoners on the strength, composition, morale, supply, and probable plans of Proctor's steadily diminishing army. As a result, he reorganized his formation, intending to personally command the primary assault on the centre of the British line with one division of his infantry arrayed in the standard "line" formation. At the same time, a second division (under Major General Joseph Desha) would swing to the left, simultaneously securing the first division's vulnerable flank from the Natives and pinning them in place, while the third division, composed of the mounted troops (under Colonel Richard Johnson), would swing down on the British right flank, rout the Natives, and then move on to exploit any breaches made by the first division infantry.

However, as he continued his advance, reports from his scouts came in with the astonishing news of Proctor's unorthodox redeployment of his troops into a quasi-light-infantry extension. Recognizing that this dispersed line gave him the opportunity of making a far more dynamic use of his cavalry, Harrison again changed his entire battle plan on the fly.

Moving his cavalry to the front, Harrison intended to make a classic cavalry charge directly at the main British line, while the infantry followed up at the double to engage any units that remained intact and secure the flanks.

However, after arriving at the field and viewing its constricted size and obstructed terrain, Colonel Richard Johnson advised an additional revision, producing a hybrid operation. This new plan called for a screen of skirmishers on foot, referred to as "spies" in later American accounts, to advance under cover of the heavy growth and open the engagement, probing for weaknesses and pinning the enemy in place. Behind this, half the mounded corps (under Colonel Richard Johnson) would move over to the American left flank and ride down on the Natives, as originally proposed. The remaining cavalry would simultaneously deploy to the American right flank (under Richard's brother, Lieutenant Colonel James Johnson) and charge the single British gun and the left flank of the now vulnerable extended British line. Once the cavalry were committed, the infantry would move up the centre and engage whatever British formations or Native opposition remained on the battlefield.[3]

* * *

ESTIMATE OF AMERICAN TROOPS, BATTLE OF THE THAMES, OCTOBER 5, 1813[3]

Twenty-Seventh Regiment: (Colonel Paul) est. 130 all ranks

Kentucky Volunteer Militia (5 brigades of infantry) (Major General Henry)

Brigadier General Trotter, est. 550 all ranks
Brigadier General King, est. 550 all ranks
Brigadier General Chiles, est. 550 all ranks
Brigadier General Allen, est. 550 all ranks
Brigadier General Caldwell, est. 550 all ranks

Kentucky Volunteer Militia (Mounted Infantry) (Colonel Johnson), est. 500 all ranks.

Artillery: 2 x 6-pounders (Major Wood), est. 30 all ranks (not used in the action)

At around 4:00 p.m. the action commenced as planned. From the very start, the British found themselves in trouble. On the British left the American advanced skirmishers, drawn from the Twenty-Seventh Regiment, used the heavy riverside undergrowth to creep forward and engage the artillery piece and its covering escort at close range. Because the horses used to haul the heavy gun and its associated limber (ammunition wagon) were requisitioned civilian mounts, and therefore entirely untrained for battlefield conditions, they panicked and bolted at the sudden noise of firing, dragging off the piece's ammunition limber. This caused the horse's handlers and parts of the associated support troops to be thrown into chaos, as they were overrun by the fleeing beasts and then dispersed as they ran after the horses in an attempt to bring them — and the vital ammunition limber — back. The gun was now completely exposed, effectively defenceless, and, apart from the single round down the barrel, without ammunition — something that Colonel Richard Johnson was not slow to take advantage of.

Signalling the charge, and with the men yelling the battle cry "Remember the Raisin!" the cavalry surged forward, overrunning the gun position, supposedly before its crew had time to even fire it the once that it could. The troopers then turned their attention to the nearby British line and, despite receiving some fire from individuals, they were not subjected to the usual withering and devastating firepower of a line volley. Nor were the foot soldiers able to gain the mutual security of forming a defensive "square." As a result, the highly vulnerable and exposed left end of the British extended formation was simply ridden down and the front line irrevocably breeched.

This was the last straw for many of the already dispirited British troops, who decided that the battle was lost and it was a case of every man for himself. A cascading rout ensued, as the already partially dispersed men abandoned the front line and headed for the woods. In the second line, watching the disintegration of the front, the remaining British troops initially stalled the American charge with a succession of ragged volleys, but thereafter also folded and commenced a disorganized retreat from the field. Lieutenant Bullock, stationed on the right flank of the British second line, later described the action:

The attack commenced about two hours after the order was given to form up across the road. I heard a heavy firing of musketry and shortly after saw our dragoons retreating together with the limber of the 6-pounder — placed on the left of the 1st line. About a minute afterwards I observed that line retreating in confusion, followed closely by the enemy's cavalry, who were galloping down the road. That portion of the 1st line which had escaped the enemy's cavalry, retreated behind the 2nd line, which stood fast, and fired an irregular volley obliquing to the right and left, which appeared to check the enemy. The line having commenced firing, my attention was directed to that part of the enemy moving directly in my front. Hearing the fire slacken, I turned towards the line and found myself [alone apart from] … three non-commissioned officers of the Grenadier company. The enemy's cavalry had advanced so close … that before a third round could be fired, they broke through the left, and the rest, not being formed to repel cavalry [i.e., in square] were compelled to retreat….[4]

— Lieutenant Bullock to
Major Frend, December 6, 1813

Stationed halfway between the two lines on the left flank, Proctor and his senior staff were not only eyewitnesses to the initial American charge on the gun, but in imminent danger of being overrun or captured. While Proctor made an initial call for his men to stand fast, the impossibility of salvaging the day was evident to his subordinates who quickly bundled their commander off the field, under hot pursuit by some of the Kentucky mounted militia.

Over on the American left flank, the cavalry attack under Lieutenant Colonel Richard Johnson had been forced to traverse the central bog in order to attack the Natives, slowing his charge. As a result, the Natives, secure in their partially protected woodland, were able to put up a more sustained and effective resistance, thereby inflicting casualties on the advancing American cavalry. Even once the British line collapsed, the Natives gamely or, perhaps more accurately, desperately, continued to fight, as they well knew their prospective fates under the unmerciful hands of the hated Kentucky militiamen. During this action, Lieutenant Colonel Johnson was wounded and unhorsed, while Tecumseh was killed (according to some subsequent accounts, by Johnson). Unable to overwhelm the Natives in the thick underbrush, most of the cavalrymen dismounted and continued the fight on foot, engaging in point-blank musket duels and hand-to-hand combat with the equally determined Natives — with no quarter given on either side. As the previously uncommitted infantry formations moved up in support, elements of the American left flank joined in the fighting through the swamp, forcing the Natives, through sheer numbers and firepower, to first retire and then abandon the contest — but not before recovering and spiriting away the body of their revered leader. Some later accounts by Kentucky militiamen claim that following the battle, strips of skin and even body parts of the fallen chief were taken directly from his corpse. This contention has, however, always been steadfastly refuted by the descendents of the Native warriors who fought at his side that day.

For Proctor, the sudden reality of his predicament hit home with a vengeance. His army was

From Pictorial Field Book of the War of 1812.

An artist's later impression of the Shawnee war Chief Tecumseh (Leaping Panther), the lynchpin of the first Native nations' alliance with the British, killed at the Battle of the Thames (Moravianstown).

American pursuit was aggressively following him from the battlefield, preventing him from making any efforts to rally his dispersed forces. Eventually, Proctor was forced to abandon his accompanying cumbersome command carriage and escape on horseback, leaving behind the spoils of victory, including a spare hat, sword, and personal chest of letters from his wife. Items that were picked up and later grandly displayed by one of his pursuers.

Late that night, Proctor and his staff arrived at Delaware, forty miles (64 kilometers) from the field of action, indicating just how rapid the pursuit had been. Behind him the remnants of the British baggage column, which had been carefully shepherded away from Amherstburg before the main retreat began and had always been kept as far to the front as possible, was either captured by the enemy or destroyed by its own escort. Casualties from the brief action and its immediate preliminaries are contradictory at best, especially for the British and Native contingents, but may be assessed generally as given alongside.[5]

The "Right" Division was effectively eliminated and the way was open for Harrison to attack Burlington and the Niagara frontier from the rear (west). However, that was not to be. Although the Americans advanced into Moravianstown, they contented themselves with looting it of anything that was considered valuable or useful, nailed

routed and dispersed, his Native allies were fleeing in unknown directions. His carefully orchestrated campaign to deliver an effective fighting force to Vincent at Burlington was in tatters. He and his staff were in imminent danger of capture, as the

ESTIMATE OF CASUALTIES, BATTLE OF THE THAMES, (MORAVIANSTOWN), OCTOBER 5, 1813[5]

British

Killed:	est. 18–25 other ranks
Wounded:	est. 25–40 other ranks
Missing/Prisoners:	est. 600 all ranks (including those taken during the retreat from Sandwich)

British Native Allies

Killed:	est. 33–100 warriors
Wounded:	unknown

American

Killed:	est. 15–20 all ranks
Wounded:	est. 30–50 all ranks

down or not, before torching the settlement and retreating to Sandwich, systematically looting and torching virtually every settlement and house on the way. Why Harrison failed to capitalize on his stunning victory over Proctor's troops and the destruction of the Native alliance, not to mention killing the man who posed the greatest individual threat to the American war effort in the west (Tecumseh), is not clearly evident. However, the combination of

- the lateness of the season and the evident approach of winter weather
- the small number of regular troops in his current force
- the lack of an established series of supply bases along his line of march
- the potential threat that the currently dispersed Natives might regroup and threaten or attack his supply lines
- the fact that his militias had originally enlisted under a sixty-day service limit, which was nearly expired

may have persuaded Harrison that his optimum action was retreat to Sandwich, to officially disband his militias and collect the bulk of his regular forces before determining what his next moves should be.

On October 16, 1813, Harrison imposed an armistice upon the subdued Native tribes that had, only a few months earlier, been berating Proctor for his lack of aggression and baying for the opportunity to strike a blow against their enemy. Harrison then consolidated the American occupation of the Detroit corridor by establishing garrison posts on both sides of the river. Finally, on October 23rd, with a contingent of 1,300 regular troops, Harrison boarded Perry's fleet for transportation down Lake Erie to Buffalo, where he intended to unite with the armies on the Niagara and press the campaign on that flank.

* * *

For the British, the news of Barclay's defeat and the loss of the entire Lake Erie fleet represented a total shift in the balance of power and control of the upper Great Lakes. The Garrison at Michilimackinac (Mackinac) was effectively cut off, and the only surviving vestige of British naval power on the upper lakes was the tiny vessel *Nancy*, which had been detached from the main fleet prior to the battle to deliver winter supplies to the isolated garrison. When this news was followed by word of Proctor's defeat, it triggered a cascade panic among the civilian and Native communities along the Grand River, who believed themselves targeted for attack and destruction should Harrison advance, as expected, on Burlington Heights.

The garrison posts at Long Point and Turkey Point were abandoned, leaving the region undefended and entirely exposed, while the commander at Burlington Heights made preparations to evacuate his post and destroy its vital supplies at the first sign of an American force approaching his station. This situation was initially caused by unfounded rumours, but thereafter compounded by the behaviour of Lieutenant John Riffenstein, the adjutant of Colonel Warburton. This officer had fled the field at Morravianstown,

possibly even as the action had commenced, and brought with him exaggerated tales and outright lies about the nature and circumstances of the defeat of Proctor. Reaching the settlements on the Grand River, he continued to spread his lies. That is, until other survivors began to filter in, bringing their own stories that blatantly contradicted Riffelstein's. However, instead of retracting or otherwise mitigating his already damaging testimonies, Riffelstein, in direct contravention of his orders to remain and assist Proctor in the rebuilding of a defence line along the Grand River, claimed his "ill" health required that he retire a "short" distance from the new British front line to obtain medical assistance. In fact, this short distance amounted to travelling through Ancaster, York, Kingston, and Prescott, to Montreal. All the while repeating and elaborating on his vitriolic perjuries. He even assumed a false identity in order to escape detention when his credibility and stories were questioned by the garrison commander at Kingston. The damage this officer caused to the war effort cannot be underestimated, as it persuaded de Rottenburg to make plans to abandon Upper Canada entirely, while Prevost initially issued highly critical public General Orders and wrote misleading confidential reports to Earl Bathurst, entirely based on this one source of malicious falsehood.

CHAPTER 8

Hard Choices

Arriving at the Grand River, General Proctor took no time for self-pity, excuses, or recriminations. Instead, he immediately set about neutralizing Riffelstein's lies by ordering the Long Point posts reoccupied as the southern anchor of a new line of defence, centred on the Grand River and manned by the miniscule force of 10 officers and 228 other ranks that he was able to cobble together during the following days.[1] Proctor also coordinated a new defensive strategy with General Vincent that would create a defensive "box," defined by a line of positions that roughly followed the Grand River/Long Point (west flank), the Lake Ontario shoreline (north), the Niagara River (east), and the Lake Erie shoreline (south).

However, as the dejected remnants of the Right Division continued to arrive at the Grand River and Burlington, they were soon followed by a flood of not only military dependents and refugee settlers but also over 1,000 homeless Native warriors and their dependants. As a result, the commissariat system at the Head-of-the Lake (Hamilton) found itself burdened to the point of collapse and was unable to feed or house most of those desperately seeking aid. Inevitably, increased numbers of reports arose of ugly incidents and clashes between the locals and their unwelcome guests, as thefts of foodstuffs began to mount. In addition, the news of American successes once again roused local American sympathizers, who stirred up discontent amongst the wavering elements of the populace. In the face of these cumulative problems, and unduly influenced by the lies spread by Riffelstein, Sir George Prevost and General de Rottenburg decided that the only logical recourse was to entirely abandon Upper Canada as far as Kingston and make preparations to withdraw down the St. Lawrence as far as Montreal if conditions worsened. In contrast, both General Proctor and General Vincent were of the determined opinion that by digging in their heels and toughing it out, they could survive until the fortunes of war smiled on them once again. In particular, Vincent put forward the argument that if a retreat was made on the Niagara frontier, disaster would probably ensue because:

- Recent heavy rains had ruined the network of local roads and trails, thereby seriously hindering any orderly withdrawal.
- Withdrawing by boat was not a viable option, as all seaworthy craft had already been taken to transport de Rottenburg and his troops to Kingston, leaving behind nothing but a collection of rotten and leaky hulks. Even if these vessels had been fully serviceable, they would still have been insufficient to simultaneously remove the over 800 sick troops and the stockpiles of munitions and supplies that had been laboriously hauled up during the previous months.
- Destroying these supplies, or leaving behind his sick and wounded, were equally unacceptable options. He could not destroy the supplies and still feed his army in an overland retreat, and leaving wounded behind would have a devastating effect on the troops' morale.
- Any retreat would expose General Proctor to attack on two fronts, just as he was beginning to re-establish his own front line.
- A second British retreat, coming so soon after Proctor's loss of the western frontier would almost certainly destroy what little loyalty remained within the Native and civilian populations.

On the other hand, by maintaining his advanced positions on the Niagara, his army was now in danger of being attacked from every point on the compass:

- From the west — if Harrison's troops advanced once more along the Thames River, overwhelmed Proctor's tissue-thin line, and captured Burlington Heights.
- From the north — if Chauncey and his fleet on Lake Ontario brought troops back from Sackets Harbor or ferried them from the east bank of the Niagara River to land at any point along the Lake Ontario shore.
- From the east — if the American troops at Fort George made a renewed offensive.
- From the south — if the American fleet, having total control of Lake Erie, landed an attack

force somewhere along the Lake Erie shoreline between the Grand River and Long Point.

Finally, there was the internal threat of the increasing unrest of his own Grand River Native allies, who, despite the presence of Proctor and his small surviving force, were in distinct danger of favouring their own interests by switching sides in an attempt to persuade the victorious Americans not to destroy their homes and farms, as had already happened to the western tribes that had followed Proctor and were now huddled, starving and homeless, around Burlington Heights.

As a result, after consulting with Proctor to gain consensus, the two generals agreed to consolidate their resources around Burlington Heights, establish a tight perimeter of defence, and then reassess their future actions in light of further intelligence. To pre-empt the potential defection of the Grand River Natives, Vincent also issued a thinly veiled threat, implying that any further distribution of food supplies to these communities would depend entirely upon the degree of active support and cooperation he received from their chiefs and warriors.

Regrettably, once the retreat began, Vincent's fears proved well founded, as the weather and transport difficulties, not to mention the breakdown of discipline amongst the troops, made Vincent's retreat from Niagara a mirror image of Proctor's

unhappy fate, with most of the stockpiles of clothing, weapons, ammunition, and food, all brought up during the summer at enormous cost and effort, being either abandoned or destroyed.

> We had a most dreadful time from the crossroads. Upwards of 300 men were straggling upon the road, and waggons loaded with miserable objects stuck fast in mudholes, broken down and unable to ascend the hills, and the men too ill to stir hand or foot…. If the army retreats, 8000 barrels of flour besides immense stores will fall into the enemy's hands.[2]
> — Thomas G. Ridout,
> October 16, 1813

By the end of October the British army on the Niagara found itself back virtually in the same positions it had occupied the previous May, and the Niagara frontier was once again open for occupation by American troops.

CHAPTER 9

Seesaw on the Niagara: October–December 1813

With the British in retreat, Colonel Winfield Scott, the overall American commander on the Niagara frontier, had the opportunity to evict Vincent and Proctor from their enclave around Burlington Heights, eliminate the remaining British Native allies as a military threat, and possibly secure Upper Canada for the American cause. Instead, Scott considered Proctor's defeat and Vincent's withdrawal as fulfilling General Wilkinson's conditions that would allow him to relinquish his Niagara command and join the planned attack against Montreal. He therefore sent orders to Brigadier General George McClure, then leading the American forces in pursuit of the British, to break off his advance and immediately return to Fort George. In his letter to Major General Wilkinson, dated October 11th, Scott made his opinion clear about his current command:

> The enemy has treated me with neglect. He continued in his old positions until Saturday last (the 9th) when he took up his retreat on Burlington Heights, and has abandoned this whole peninsula.... The British burnt every thing in store in this neighborhood; three thousand blankets, many hundred stand of arms; also the blankets in the men's packs and every article of clothing not in actual use.... It was first reported ... that these regiments had marched to support Proctor.... I am pretty sure, however, that they are gone below... hence I

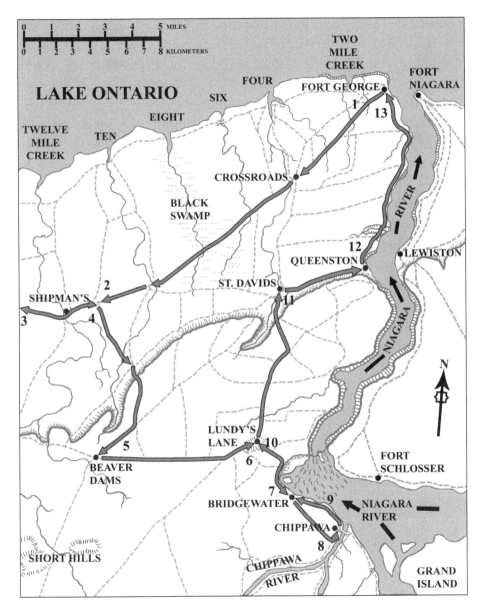

MCCLURE'S MARCH OF DESTRUCTION, OCTOBER 10–13TH, 1813

1. Brigadier General McClure's force departs Fort George on October 10th.

2. Finding the roads obstructed, the American passage is slowed.

3. Somewhere beyond Shipman's Corners the American advance grinds to a halt.

4. Receiving orders to abandon the advance and return to Newark, McClure diverts south from the main road back to Fort George.

5–12. Passing through the region, McClure and his troops ransack and loot communities and individual homes indiscriminately, as well as taking "prisoners" without providing any just cause or official charges.

13. McClure's force returns to Fort George on October 13th.

have no difficulty in concluding that all of the movements of the enemy will concentrate at Kingston.... Chapin, who has been commissioned Lieutenant Colonel, marched late last evening up the lake with about one hundred volunteers under his command. And was followed this morning by ... McClure and Porter, with about one thousand men, Indians and militia included. There is no danger of their coming up with the enemy or they would be in great danger of a total annihilation ... many of the militia left ... with the avowed design of plunder.... My position has become truly insupportable, without the possibility of an attack at this post, and without the possibility of reaching you with time enough to share in the glory of impending operations below.[1]

Meanwhile, General McClure was close to giving up the chase, as he found that the retreating British had demolished every bridge and felled trees to block the roads, making his army's advance impossible until the way was cleared. However, after receiving Scott's orders to return to Fort George, instead of returning the way he had come, he led his men on a circuitous route via Beaver Dams, Lundy's

Lane, Chippawa, St. Davids, and Queenston; looting homes of their valuables, seizing their livestock, and killing any remaining animals that could not be taken along with the column. His force also wantonly rendered buildings uninhabitable by destroying their doors and windows. Even his own militia subordinates, Brigadier General Peter B. Porter and Lieutenant Colonel Cyrenius Chapin, became embarrassed by this tactic, as Chapin later recorded:

> The march of McClure from Beaver Dams to Queenston will long be remembered by the distressed victims. Property of almost every description was plundered and buildings burned under the general's own eye.[2]

Returning to Fort George on October 13th, McClure's column not only contained his accumulated loot but also a host of "prisoners," consisting principally of prominent civilians, paroled militiamen, and Natives, all of whom were incarcerated in Fort Niagara without McClure laying any charges against them nor giving them any prospect of a trial. Within hours of McClure's arrival, an impatient Colonel Scott had transferred his command, ferried his troops across the Niagara, and begun his march to Sackets Harbor. In the days that followed, although "the roads were in an almost impassable state, yet a forced march was maintained during some fourteen days, during which it rained nearly every day and the sun was seldom seen."[3]

Hearing that Wilkinson's St. Lawrence campaign had been delayed, Scott urged his marching men on, determined to join the expedition. Exhausted, sickly, and footsore, Scott's men were within thirty miles (50 kilometres) of Sackets Harbor when their column met Secretary of War Armstrong's cavalcade returning to Washington. Informing Scott that Wilkinson had finally departed and begun his campaign, Armstrong ordered that the column should continue onto Sackets Harbor, there to enter winter quarters and recuperate. However, Winfield Scott was determined that *he* at least would not be denied his share of the glory of the attack on Montreal. Therefore, instead of tending to the needs of his exhausted troops, he pressured Armstrong into giving him permission to turn over his men into the care of his subordinates, while he rode off in hot pursuit of Wilkinson's army. After an exhausting cross-country ride, Scott finally caught up with Wilkinson near Ogdensburg, whereupon he "wangled" a new command for himself with the advance force of the flotilla.

Back on the Niagara, at the end of October General Harrison arrived at Fort George with his 1,300 regulars brought from the Detroit frontier. Together with McClure's 1,300 troops and around 400 Native allies, they planned to seize Burlington Heights and smash the British enclave. At the same time, a smaller secondary force under Brigadier General Porter would move out from Fort Erie and sweep west along the adjacent shoreline to distract the British attention and threaten the Grand River Native communities. On November 17th Harrison's division sailed from Newark aboard a number of Chauncey's vessels, before anchoring off the Twelve Mile Creek to await McClure's force advancing along the shoreline. However, the following day a strong gale blew up, forcing the vessels to disperse and run before the storm rather than be wrecked on a lee shore. Without Harrison's regular infantry to stiffen his resolve, McClure abandoned the expedition and retreated back to Fort George. At the same time, Porter's sortie from Fort Erie failed to materialize, and only a small raiding force actually went on a marauding sweep toward the Long Point area. This was intercepted and defeated by a detachment of the local Norfolk militia, who had been embodied the previous month when the regular garrisons had temporarily withdrawn and had then ignored Proctor's orders to disband when the regular had returned, as they were determined to continue to defend their homes and communities against all threats.

Once the scattered American fleet reassembled off Fort Niagara, any renewal of offensive

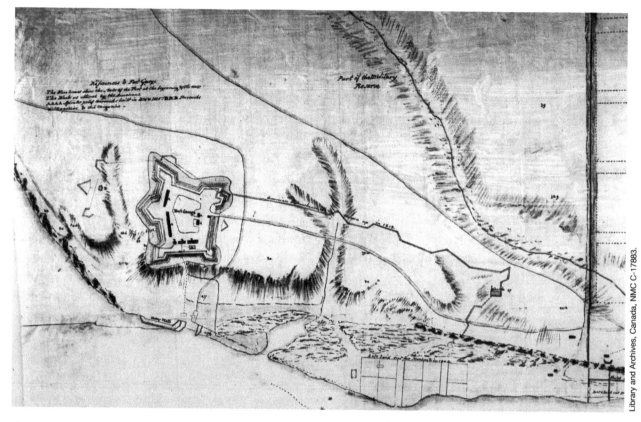

Library and Archives, Canada, NMC C-17883.

Fort George and its adjacent defensive earthworks, as the Americans left it late in 1813.

operations was precluded by new orders from General Wilkinson directing that Harrison's troops be shipped directly to Sackets Harbor as quickly as possible to support the St. Lawrence campaign. Before leaving, Harrison transferred command of the Niagara back to McClure, but made a recommendation that was to later prove highly embarrassing to himself and the United States army.

> The orders which you heretofore have received will govern you. It will be necessary that you keep a vigilant eye over the

disaffected part of the inhabitants, and I recommend that you make use of the zeal, activity and local knowledge which Colonel Willcocks certainly possesses to counteract the machinations of our enemy, and ensure the confidence of our friends among the inhabitants. It will however … be your wish, as it is your duty, to guard the latter as much as possible from oppression.

(15 November 1813)[4]

Taking Harrison's advice, McClure appointed Willcocks and his "Canadian Volunteers" as the effective "police" for controlling the local population, but entirely ignored Wilkinson's call for their supervision. As a result, these men began a new round of reprisals by "arresting" anyone connected with the Upper Canada Legislature or Canadian militia command and intimidating into silence those who dared voice any dissent over their actions. As this reign of force grew, so did the retaliation of the local populace, resulting in an escalation of the level of violence being meted out by both sides in this miniature "civil war."

To replace Harrison's troops, McClure initially attempted to mobilize additional U.S. militia troops. In this he was not merely unsuccessful, but there were increasing signs that his current troops would refuse to undertake any further offensive operations once their term of enlistment ended. In fact, over the following weeks the American garrison began to wither away, as individuals, detachments, and whole companies unilaterally crossed the river to the United States as their enlistment periods expired. Consequently, despite repeated promises of financial reward for those who re-enlisted and threats of trial and dishonour for those who quit the field, McClure's force dwindled to less than 600 men by the end of the month.

At Burlington, buoyed by the collapse of the American advance and with the arrival of news from the Lower Province that the American invasion down the St. Lawrence had been utterly defeated (for details see Chapter 10), British plans for the abandonment of Upper Canada were reversed. New orders arrived from de Rottenburg for the improvement of defensive positions and the construction of barracks and storehouses at Burlington Heights to accommodate and feed the huge number of dependant refugees from the western end of the colony. By the end of November, the pendulum was again swinging in favour of the British. On November 29th, the British outposts at Stoney Creek heard that Willcocks was out on a raid near Forty Mile Creek. In response, a small detachment from the Incorporated Militia were sent to intercept him and almost succeeded

Library and Archives Canada, C-040034.

Facing page:

1) *Fort Niagara, NY, from the Canadian side*, J.P. Cockburn, artist, 1829. The Fort George garrison common and Butler's Barracks complex (right). The American Fort Niagara can be seen across the river (upper left centre).

Modern views of the reconstructed and restored buildings associated with the war in and around Newark (Niagara-on-the-Lake).

(2–4) The Butlers Barracks complex.

(5) Navy Hall.

BRITISH FORCE, ADVANCE ON FORT GEORGE, DECEMBER 12, 1813 [5]

(Colonel Murray)
Royal Artillery (Lieutenant Charlton), 1 x 6-pounder, 1 x 5½ inch Howitzer, 20 rank and file
19th Light Dragoons (Cornet Horton), 25 rank and file
Provincial Dragoons (Captain Merritt), 14 rank and file
100th Regiment (Lieutenant Colonel Hamilton), 340 rank and file
Incorporated Militia (Captain Kerby), 20 rank and file
Militia Volunteers (Captain Caldwell, Captain Wilson), 80 rank and file
Western Native allies (Lieutenant Colonel Elliott), 70 warriors

in capturing the renegade leader. Fleeing back to the American lines, Willcocks and his men spread tales of a wholesale British advance. This prompted McClure to withdraw his forces back toward the Twenty Mile Creek, which finally encouraged General Vincent to approve a general forward movement by an advance corps under Colonel Murray.[5]

Advancing across the snow-covered ground in a fleet of sleighs, Murray's advance caught up with Willcocks near the Twenty Mile Creek on December 10th. In a brief firefight, Willcocks' men were routed and fled to Fort George, where their reports spread panic amongst the remaining garrison troops. Overnight, desertions increased to the point where the American Native allies outnumbered the men of the army detailed to guard the post. McClure now faced the prospect of either trying to hold his position with sixty regular troops, forty militia volunteers, and around seventy Native allies, or retreating back across the river after destroying the reconstructed Fort George, along with large stockpiles of supplies and tents left behind by the regular army. Instead, he did neither, opting instead to burn Newark before decamping across the river.

McClure subsequently claimed these actions were officially sanctioned in writing by Secretary of War Armstrong. Armstrong retorted that he had authorized such action *only* in the event of a British attack *and* subject to the condition that the act would improve the active defences of the fort. Armstrong also claimed to have specifically instructed McClure to give adequate previous notice to the inhabitants in order to allow them to remove their possessions. Instead, sending notice that the town would be put to the torch without delay, McClure delegated the distasteful job to Willcocks and his men, who proceeded to carry it out without a qualm. In the teeth of a strong winter storm, Newark's few remaining citizens were herded into the streets and watched as their homes were reduced to ashes. Fortunately a few outlying barns and sheds in the surrounding fields remained unscathed, allowing most of the distressed refugees to huddle in what little shelter could be found, while others fled west to seek refuge with the advancing British forces.

As the first of the homeless civilians reached Murray's troops, word of the atrocity spread like wildfire. Desperate for news of their families, the

The main barracks within the modern reconstruction of Fort George in winter. Restored to its pre-war configuration as part of a 1930s make-work program, it is now a Parks Canada National Heritage Site.

men of the militias from around Newark called for an immediate advance, which was taken up by the entire body of troops, regardless of the threat of attack from the American garrison. Seething with fury, the avenging troops descended on Newark to find it still burning and the militiamen's families destitute: "Nothing but heaps of coals and the streets full of furniture that the inhabitants were fortunate enough to get out of their houses met the eye in all directions...."[6]

On approach to the fort the fortifications initially appeared intact and fully ready for defence. But on closer inspection the gates were found open and the garrison gone. The main arsenal of powder and ammunition had been burnt, but several smaller magazines were untouched, leaving behind a valuable supply of powder. The fort's gun batteries were devoid of their cannon barrels, but the carriages remained undamaged. The initial thought was that the retreating Americans had taken the barrels across the river, but the following morning a search revealed that most had simply been tipped into the fort ditches. The most valuable discovery was that most of the barracks and enough tents to accommodate almost 1,500 men were standing intact and could be used for the relief of the homeless civilians. The next day detachments were sent out to scour the frontier and apprehend any American stragglers. Coming

under fire from the batteries at Lewiston, the infuriated British and Canadian troops watched as some of the buildings at Queenston were ignited by "hot-shot." The Americans now appeared determined to randomly lay waste to everything on the west bank, and calls for revenge rose from the militiamen.

The following day, Captain James Kerby, commanding a company of Incorporated Militia and a party of Natives, reached Fort Erie in sleighs, just in time to catch the last of the fort garrison abandoning their position and retreating to boats on the riverbank. Without hesitation the militiamen and Natives fired and then swept down on the hapless Americans with bayonet and hatchet, killing several and capturing over twenty men. However, those fortunate enough to push off from the shore were not immune, as a fusillade of shots caused additional casualties before the retreating troops could pull out of range. While the Canadian side of the Niagara River was firmly back in British hands, calls arose that it was time to take the war to the far bank. The Americans should get a taste of their own medicine for a change.

Under all the previous administrations of Upper Canada, the policies of defence had remained virtually unchallenged since the death of Brock, but now Lieutenant General Gordon Drummond was announced as the new hand at the helm of Upper Canada's war effort, and he was not interested in awaiting the Americans' next move. This change in command had been prompted by a succession of events that had taken place the previous month on the St. Lawrence frontier. There, the grandiose American plan of invasion had gone disastrously wrong from the very outset.

The restored and reconstructed main gate and barracks of Fort Erie in winter.

CHAPTER 10

The St. Lawrence Campaign: September–November 1813

Having stripped the Niagara frontier for the proposed St. Lawrence campaign, General Wilkinson's preparations were beset by repeated delays, caused in no little part by Secretary of War Armstrong's repeated interference. In addition, according to the original plan, Wilkinson's advance was to be matched by a subordinate invasion through the Lake Champlain corridor under Major General Wade Hampton. Unfortunately, Hampton and Wilkinson were sworn personal enemies. Hampton therefore sought every opportunity to undermine Wilkinson's authority, instead of co-operating in the planned two-pronged attack into Lower Canada.

By October a succession of freezing storms presaged an early winter, making the sensibility of launching an invasion so late in the season dubious at best. In fact, these storms had already wrecked over a third of the boats and caused the loss of nearly half the intended supplies during the invasion's build-up of men and materiel at Grenadier Island (located south of the confluence of Lake Ontario and the St. Lawrence River). Nonetheless, neither Armstrong nor Wilkinson were prepared to suffer the inevitable political and public censure that would follow if the invasion was abandoned, or even postponed until the spring.

The invasion commenced on September 19, 1813, when General Wade Hampton's army of over 3,500 troops advanced from its base at Plattsburgh (New York), fully expecting to meet up with Wilkinson's forces on the banks of the St. Lawrence River. Instead, almost immediately after crossing the border into Lower Canada, Hampton found the roads had been blockaded and bridges burned. His advance also ran into a small defensive detachment blocking the way at Odelltown, resulting in a minor skirmish. Although he could easily have swept aside this paltry opposition, Hampton revised his plan of campaign on the spot and marched his force back across the border to Chazy before pushing hurriedly west, with the goal of making up the lost time by passing up alongside the Châteauguay River to reach the St. Lawrence River opposite Coteau-du-Lac. After a horrendous journey along dilapidated muddy trackways, Hampton's columns finally reached the head of the Châteauguay River at Four Corners. However, here he received word of Wilkinson's stalled departure, along with orders to stop and await further developments before proceeding with his own invasion. Infuriated and blaming Wilkinson for his predicament, but unable to do otherwise, Hampton ordered a fortified camp built and waited.

As the delay extended from days to weeks, Hampton found himself faced with the reality of seeing his muster rolls shrinking dramatically, not only through deaths from sickness and disease but also desertions. There were also increased reports of insubordination and near-mutinies occurring in every regiment. Consequently, after receiving intelligence on October 21st that the enemy on his proposed line of march were principally Lower Canadian militia and a few Native allies, Hampton decided enough was enough. Ignoring Armstrong's directives to coordinate any attack, and probably tempted by the prospect of stealing Wilkinson's thunder with an easy victory, Hampton ordered an immediate advance. Marching once again along heavily rutted and muddy lanes, and under conditions of driving freezing rain, Hampton's army quickly brushed aside the first outlying pickets of the British forces and advanced to a point some forty miles (60 kilometers) southwest of Montreal. There, on October 26th, they came up against the enemy's first real line of defence, consisting of a wall of trees felled across the road and manned by enemy troops.

This front line was composed of about 400 men (from a total defence force of less than 1,800) and was indeed principally Lower Canadian militia and Native allies, but backed by a well-trained unit of Canadian Fencible Infantry, all under the command of an experienced military commander, Colonel Charles de Salaberry (Canadian Voltigeurs). Warned well in advance of Hampton's advance, de Salaberry's troops had constructed a succession of prepared defences that blocked the road. Secure behind these works and flanked on the one side by dense bush and swamps and on the other by the unfordable river, de Salaberry and his small force in the front line were able to beat off repeated American attacks during the course of the day. In fact, so successful were these defences that the three supporting lines of defences and troops never engaged the enemy.

Unable to evict this significantly smaller Canadian force, Hampton's army finally retired from the field to consider its options. Despite maintaining a significant advantage in numbers of troops and supporting artillery, as well as being capable of taking another route to link up with Wilkinson, Hampton assembled his council of officers and announced his determination to retreat back to his base at the Four Corners. Following a raucous meeting, and against the strident objections of several of his senior officers, Hampton steadfastly refused to continue the campaign, thus crippling the American invasion plan and leaving Wilkinson without the vital supplies and manpower he fully expected to have.

Not knowing of this disaster, Wilkinson's own invasion finally began on November 3rd, when the American fleet of over 300 vessels began their passage down the St. Lawrence River loaded with over 8,000 troops and crews. Behind them a separate squadron remained on Lake Ontario with orders to blockade Kingston and prevent de Rottenburg from sending any forces in pursuit to attack the Americans from behind. After arriving at French Creek (Clayton, NY) and rendezvousing with additional troops and boats, the expedition recommenced. But within hours, all of the preplanning disintegrated into chaos as the supposedly rigid divisions of vessels became intermixed amongst the narrow, winding channels of the Thousand Islands

From Pictorial Field Book of the War of 1812.

A later rendition of Wilkinson's flotilla passing through the Thousand Islands region at the beginning of the St. Lawrence campaign against Montreal.

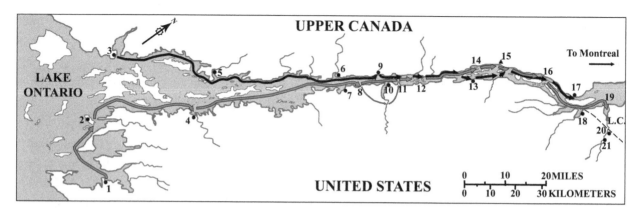

THE COURSE OF THE ST. LAWRENCE CAMPAIGN, OCTOBER–NOVEMBER 1813

1. Sackets Harbor. The main American force is assembled at Sackets Harbor throughout September and October.

2. Grenadier Island. American forces begin their transfer to Grenadier Island on October 16th. They leave beginning on November 2nd to sail down the St. Lawrence River.

3. Kingston. The British "Corps of Observation" eventually leaves Kingston to shadow the American force on November 7th.

4. French Creek (Clayton, NY). After a short initial passage, the American flotilla reaches French Creek on November 3rd, linking up with additional troops. The enlarged flotilla leaves on November 5th but becomes disordered in the passage of the Thousand Islands region, forcing another reassembly at Morrisburg (7).

5. Gananoque.

6. Elizabethtown/Brockville.

7. Morrisburg (Morrisville, NY).

8. Troops from the American army are landed above Ogdensburg and march around the village during the night of November 6/7, while the boats make a passage down the river in an attempt to pass undetected.

9. Prescott. After firing on the American boats during the night of November 6/7, the garrison at Prescott prepares to follow the Americans downriver when the "Corps of Observation" flotilla arrives on November 8th. The enlarged flotilla leaves Prescott on November 9th.

10. Ogdensburg.

11. The American Army re-boards its flotilla below Ogdensburg on the morning of November 7th.

12. Gallop Rapids. The American flotilla passes the Gallop Rapids on November 7th. The British follow through on November 9th.

13. Hamilton (Waddington, NY). British boats attack and a landing party temporarily occupies the village on the morning of November 10th.

14. Rapids du Plat. The American flotilla passes the rapids on November 9th, the British follow through on November 10th.

15. The Crysler's Farm battlefield.

16. Long Sault Rapids. Following the battle the American flotilla passes through on November 12th, the British follow on November 15th.

17. Cornwall.

18. St. Regis. The planned rendezvous point for Wilkinson's and Hampton's armies.

19. Salmon River. The American flotilla discharges its troops on November 13/14 and boats are scuttled within the river to block any British pursuit.

20. The American winter encampment on the Salmon River.

21. French Mills.

region, necessitating a further delay at Morrisburg (Morrisville) while the squadrons were reassembled. Nor did Wilkinson's problems end there, as the flotilla continued to suffer difficulties in its passage downriver, including the spoilage and loss of significant amounts of food and ammunition supplies stored in leaking boats that were forced to fall out of formation to make repairs.

Downriver, at Prescott, the garrison's commander, Lieutenant Colonel Pearson, was aware of the two-pronged American build-up, and had been preparing his troops for a fight should either American force come within reach. All that remained was to see that his garrison was not caught unawares. To this end, on October 13th, the entire Prescott garrison was put on a twenty-four-hour alert. "As the enemy have made their appearance on the frontier, Lieutenant Colonel Pearson … orders that every man will sleep in his accoutrements, ready to turn out at a moments warning. The men to be outfitted with arms, flints and ammunition…."[1] This meant that each man would be attempting to sleep while wearing his full uniform, including boots and gaiters, as well as his fully loaded leather cartridge box on its cross-belt and bayonet/cross-belt combination.

With the news of the Allied victory at Châteauguay, the American threat on that flank was eliminated. In response, Lieutenant Colonel Pearson made preparations to take his regular troops into action, or at least to move at the shortest possible notice to support the garrison at Kingston if the threatened American attack from Sackets Harbor fell there. However, he also hedged his bets, assessing that Montreal might be the ultimate American target. Fortunately, countering this threat did not require any troop movements, as his

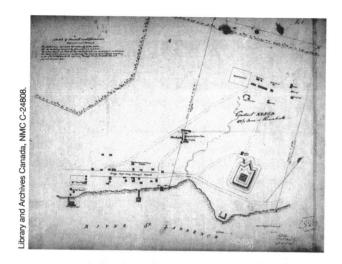

Library and Archives Canada, NMC C-24808.

An 1816 map showing the military strongpoint (later named Fort Wellington), associated military buildings, and the village of Prescott.

garrison could simply wait for the enemy to come to them. What *was* required was sufficient early warning. In response, Lieutenant Colonel Pearson chose an officer from the Incorporated Militia to undertake this important duty:

> To Lieutenant Clark, Incorporated Militia,
> 1 November 1813
>
> Sir, You will immediately proceed to Elliot's where you will take up your station with a view of watching the navigation of the river and strictly ascertaining the nature of all crafts passing down with troops and scows containing horses, artillery, etc. or should anything else suffer to lead you to suppose the enemy is passing down to Prescott, or the neighbourhood, or should they be seen in any situation, you will instantly take horse and repair to Prescott with all possible diligence, alerting the country as you pass down.
>
> T. Pearson
> Lieutenant Colonel, Commanding[2]

After waiting at Elliot's farm (five miles upriver from Elizabethtown/Brockville) for three days and nights

> … at an early hour of the forenoon, an advance guard of [enemy] vessels hove in sight. Lt. Clark promptly took possession of a farmer's horse and in a few minutes rode into Brockville on his foam covered steed and announced "the enemy are at hand." With only a moment's pause, he dashed away for Prescott with the report for his commanding officer….[3]

At Prescott, although the garrison was immediately put on full alert and every cannon primed to engage the American fleet once it came within range, nothing took place during the following two days. This was because, having received detailed reports of the strength of Prescott's defences and manned readiness, Wilkinson was unwilling to hazard his army on making a direct assault on that post. Instead, on the night of November 6/7th, the bulk of the American army was disembarked a few miles upriver to march, in complete silence, in a wide detour around Ogdensburg before returning to the riverbank to meet up with their boats. At the same time, under cover of the darkness, the emptied American flotilla attempted to float undetected past Prescott by using a haze of fog and hugging the dark cover of the American shoreline — an attempt that failed.

Once the American boats were detected, a barrage of fire, lasting over three hours, was laid on the dimly visible, low-in-the-water shapes, over 1,800 yards (1,646 meters) away. According to later official American accounts, the long column of boats suffered negligible damage and casualties in their successful passage. On the other hand, according to local histories, at least two boats were reported to have been deliberately run aground and abandoned by their panicked crews, while others were holed badly enough that they had to be beached for temporary repairs and then leave large portions of their cargos at Ogdensburg. Having succeeded in bypassing Prescott, the American army re-boarded their transports and continued downriver toward the Gallop Rapids, the first in a series of dangerous navigational obstacles that had to be traversed during the descent.

On November 7th news of Hampton's defeat at Châteauguay reached Wilkinson, causing consternation and a rapid reassessment of the viability of the entire campaign. In response, Wilkinson dispatched orders for Hampton and his command to make a new rendezvous at St. Regis, near Cornwall. The appearance of 200 men from the 1st Dundas embodied militia (Captain John Munroe), supported by a small detachment of Natives, persuaded Wilkinson that if he was to continue downriver and pass the rapids safely, his vulnerable northern flank needed securing. For this job, Wilkinson landed a strong force of around 1,100 troops under Colonel Alexander Macomb and the newly arrived Colonel Winfield Scott, who soon forced the substantially smaller Canadian unit and Natives to retire eastward.

With the riverbank secured from attack, the flotilla spent the remainder of the day "shooting" the rapids. However, once below, and while the landing parties were re-boarding, another small detachment of the enemy's light artillery and embodied militia appeared on the road and opened fire on the boats. This detachment had been forwarded post

Contemporary (2012) views taken from the 1812 earthwork ramparts of Fort Wellington. The current centre blockhouse is a post-war replacement of the original. To the south, beyond the river, lie the United States and the town of Ogdensburg.

haste by Lieutenant Colonel Pearson from Prescott, for the express purpose of delaying the Americans long enough for Pearson to arrive to give battle. In response, detachments of Colonel Forsyth's riflemen were re-landed and advanced on the gun and militiamen, who wisely withdrew after having fulfilled their objective of delaying the Americans for an hour or so.

Back at Prescott, after forwarding the advanced unit, Lieutenant Colonel Pearson ordered the immediate mobilization of the bulk of the garrison, intending to make a forced march in pursuit as soon as possible. Instead, the following day (November 8, 1813) a flotilla of boats, packed with around 800 troops, arrived from Kingston. This "Corps of Observation"[4] had been rapidly put together at Kingston once news of the American movements down the St. Lawrence had been confirmed. After evading the detection of Chauncey's naval blockade on the upper reaches of the St. Lawrence River, this corps was now shadowing the Americans with the intent of attacking them if an advantageous opportunity arose. Under the overall command of Lieutenant Colonel Joseph Morrison (89th Regiment), the naval force was commanded by Captain William Mulcaster (R.N).

Determined to participate in the upcoming action, Lieutenant Colonel Pearson made a proposal Morrison could not refuse by offering to join the pursuit with his already prepared strike force.[*5] The resulting addition of seven gunboats and sixty bateaux, as well as the troops and a select body of knowledgeable pilots and crews, brought Morrison's command to around 1,200–1,300 men in total.

Aboard the American flotilla, General Wilkinson's health was now in serious question as he was unable to fulfill his daily duties. Official reports recorded this as an "indisposition of General Wilkinson that rendered him incapable of taking the field,"[6] which some sympathetic historians later put down to an overuse of the drug laudanum to counteract a bout of dysentery, but by at least one sworn account of the day was described in a less complementary manner.

"CORPS OF OBSERVATION"[4]

49th Regiment (Lieutenant Colonel Charles
    Plenderleath), 8 companies, est. 325 all ranks
89th Regiment (Major Miller Clifford), 8 companies,
    est. 475 all ranks
Lord Beresford (schooner)
Sir Sydney Smith (schooner)
7 gunboats
Unknown number of bateaux

… we halted at a small house near the river, and while there discovered a boat approaching the shore. Major Forsyth hailed the crew, and on explanation was informed it was General Wilkinson's boat. The Major, myself, and others, met the General at the waters edge, and asked if he wished to come on shore. Indicating that he did, Forsyth and myself took him by the arms to assist him out of the boat,

PRESCOTT CONTINGENT

(Lieutenant Colonel Thomas Pearson)[5]
49th Regiment, flank companies (2 companies)
    (Lieutenant Samuel Holland), est. 90 all ranks
Canadian Fencible Regiment (2 companies) (not
    known), est. 120 all ranks
Lower Canada Voltigeur Regiment (3 companies)
    (Captain Jacques Adhémar, Captain William
    Johnson, Captain Jacques Herse), est. 165 all
    ranks
Royal Artillery (3 x 6-pounder guns and crews)
    (Captain Henry Jackson), est. 60 all ranks
Provincial Light Dragoons (Captain Richard Fraser),
    est. 15 all ranks
Mohawk Native allies, est. 30 warriors
Volunteer boat crews, est. 75–125 men

and up the bank. We found him most abominably intoxicated, and hurried him into the house…. After seating him on a chair near the fire, the major and myself retired to consult what was best to be done …when we concluded to detail and post a guard near the door of the house, to keep out both citizens and soldiers.[7]

— Major Birdsall

As an overdose of Laudanum can produce similar symptoms, the exact cause of his "indisposition" cannot be proved one way or another. However, irrespective of its cause, the fact remained that the American army had a serious problem on its hands. For in spite of his incapacity, Wilkinson refused to step down and allow his second-in-command, Major General Morgan Lewis, to take control.

By the end of November 8th there were only ten days of unspoiled food remaining for the army and, frustrated by the continued harassment of small Allied detachments, Wilkinson called another council of officers to decide if the campaign should continue. At the same time, further news arrived from General Hampton that he was refusing to make any further attempt to link up with Wilkinson for an attack on Montreal. Despite this catastrophic news, and after hearing of his officers' determination to continue the campaign, Wilkinson decided to take full control of the north bank of the St. Lawrence by landing the bulk of his troops from the boats. He also transferred his cavalry and train of spare horses from the south bank to the Canadian side of the river.

November 9th was passed by both armies on the move. The Americans, led by the Second Brigade (Brigadier General Jacob Brown), supported by the "Elite" Brigade (Colonel Alexander Macomb and Colonel Winfield Scott), marched ahead of the flotilla of boats and secured the next set of rapids (the Rapids du Plat), thus allowing the boats to pass safely downriver and the army to encamp for the night alongside the farmstead of John Crysler.

From Pictorial Field Book of the War of 1812.

Brigadier General Jacob Brown, commander of the American advance forces during their campaign against Montreal.

November 10th proved to be a day of campaigning under high winds and freezing rain. The British busied themselves catching up with the enemy. For the Americans, however, things were far less simple as Wilkinson's ability to command continued to deteriorate. General Brown's advance force had marched at first light and had been augmented until it had over 2,600 men, composed of the Second Brigade, the "Elite" Brigade, the First Light Dragoon Regiment (Lieutenant Colonel Nelson Luckett), and two 6-pounder guns. Charged with clearing the Long Sault rapids of any enemy forces, their progress had been slowed by small detachments of Canadian militia who retreated only after having destroyed every bridge along the road. Some miles behind, Brigadier General John Parker Boyd, following his orders from General Wilkinson to take the bulk of the army down the riverside road to join Brown, had already marched more than two miles when the sounds of firing came from the direction of the American rearguard. After receiving reports from a detachment of the Second Dragoons sent back to reconnoitre, Boyd decided that the British were indeed making an attack, designed to hit his column from behind while on the march. As his orders had also included a clause that if the British made an attack he was to turn and fight, he countermarched his substantial force and led it back through the woods toward the

Meanwhile, Morrison's combined force, having left Prescott but without their two largest ships, had moved with all speed aboard their own flotilla until news arrived of the Americans shifting the bulk of their force to the north bank. Morrison did the same while his emptied boats continued to move in parallel on the river.

open farmland lying to the east of Crysler's Farm. Once there, noting that the redcoated troops were keeping their distance, he deployed his force into a line-of-battle and awaited developments.

For their part, the British had had a busy morning. Captain William Mulcaster and his gunboat flotilla had started the day by raiding the American village of Hamilton (Waddington, New York), before moving downriver and bombarding the American rearguard of gunboats at Cooks Point. Following an ineffectual exchange of fire between the two small flotillas at long range, Mulcaster's boats were eventually forced to withdraw upriver when the Americans added a shore battery to their firing line.

Onshore, Morrison had no intention of making a concerted attack on the vastly superior number of American troops. He instead contented himself by advancing small detachments to harass the Americans into overreacting, by sending first companies and then entire regiments back and forth across the muddy and fenced fields — thus rendering themselves as excellent targets of opportunity to the effective advance/fire/move/fire/retire tactics adopted by the British. Together, these tactics served the desired purpose of stalling the American advance yet again and simultaneously tired out the bulk of the American troops for no effective result.

Meanwhile, General Brown's 2,600-strong advance force found itself facing a contingent of some 300 men from the 1st Stormont and 2nd Glengarry Embodied Militias (under Major James Dennis [49th Regiment]) at Hoople's Creek, two miles (3.2 kilometers) above the head of the Long Sault rapids.

After burning the bridge, Dennis' militiamen had hidden along the overgrown riverbank and only opened fire as Brown's troops attempted to cross. Overestimating the forces facing him at over double their actual number, Brown brought up his artillery support and began to open fire. He also detached Colonel Winfield Scott, with his new command, to move to the left, locate a crossing point further up the creek, and outflank the enemy before them. Scott subsequently found the required crossing point, but by the time he and his force had returned downstream, Dennis and his Canadian militias had already safely withdrawn, having again achieved their objective of stalling the American advance.

With night closing in and the freezing rain continuing to fall, Boyd's formations withdrew to the landing beaches just below Cooks Point and their boats, leaving behind in the woods a strong chain of pickets. Just under three miles away, the combined forces under Morrison encamped near Crysler's Farm before continuing the contest the next morning. However, later that evening Lieutenant Colonel Morrison received an urgent dispatch from General de Rottenburg at Kingston, while Captain Mulcaster received a similar communique from Sir James Yeo.

Both contained direct orders to immediately disengage and return to Kingston to bolster the defences in the face of what was perceived as an imminent threat of attack from Sackets Harbor.

Shocked and dismayed to receive these commands, both commanders believed that the imminent danger to Montreal, coupled with the situation immediately before them (namely of holding the enemy at a location where they could bring the Americans to battle while holding the advantage of position and ground), was something that could not be abandoned. Morrison therefore called a council of officers to discuss the situation. Without hesitation, the assembled subordinates concurred, backing Morrison and Mulcaster's judgements. With that answer, both senior officers drafted replies to their respective commanders disobeying their orders — but covered themselves by sending a courier with duplicate copies of both the orders and replies, plus memoranda of their reasoning to disobey, directly to Sir George Prevost at Montreal.

They then settled down to plan how they were about to take on a force that outnumbered them approximately six to one.

CHAPTER 11

The Battle of Crysler's Farm: November 11, 1813

Under a heavily overcast and windy dawn, on November 11th the two armies prepared themselves to continue their respective plans of campaign. In the American camp, General Wilkinson remained invalided in bed aboard the fleet, but still expected to make all command decisions and was awaiting news from downriver that the way was clear to advance. His second-in-command, Major General Morgan Lewis, was also reportedly ill, but believing he was now in command was giving directions that an immediate advance was to be made, with or without the way being clear. This left the direct command of the troops in the field in the hands of Brigadier General John Boyd, who was completely in the dark about what either of his superiors had in mind.

In the British camp, Lieutenant Colonel Morrison had no intention of advancing through the intervening woods to attack the vastly larger American force on a ground of their choosing. Instead, he had made the maximum use of the available terrain to augment his defensive strategy. Comprised of an open area of farmland, roughly one mile (1.6 kilometers) wide (east-west) and half a mile (800 meters) deep (north-south), it was bordered on the south by the St. Lawrence River; the east by the dense woodland currently dividing him from the enemy; the north by an equally dense and, in areas, swampy forest; and on the west by open farmland. As a result, Morrison's northern and southern flanks were relatively secure, forcing the enemy to approach through broken and obstructed ground from the east while, in the event of a setback, his own line of retreat westward was open and clear. Within the open ground, there were additional

From *The Day of Crysler's Farm.*

Brigadier General John Boyd, commander of the American Forces in the Battle of Crysler's Farm.

of his own encampment, giving him an additional line of escape if required. The open fields, running inland in a series of parallel strips from the river, were bordered by chest-high split-rail wooden fences that made excellent defensive obstacles,while the saturated ground was composed of muddy ploughed acreages, interspersed with dormant arable pasture and late crops of wheat. While the ground was relatively flat, it did contain an elevation gradient that dropped from west to east, giving Morrison the slight advantage of height for his artillery. Finally, toward the east end of the open fields, the diffident drainage of the area had created three distinct watercourses that cut into the fields, each running roughly north from the river and containing a small meandering creek and adjacent

A split-rail "snake" fence marking a field boundary. These obstacles played an important role in impeding the movements of both armies during the course of the battle.

features that benefited his strategies. The only east-west road ran immediately above the steep and muddy riverbank that could be swept by his own artillery on land or from Mulcaster's gunboats in the river. The only north-south line of communication, known as Nine-Mile Road, was directly in front boggy ground. These obstacles ranged from the shallow, curved "west gully," through the shorter but deeper "centre gully," to the wide and deep field-long "east ravine" that stood around 150 yards (137 meters) from the eastern treeline. Together these three water channels effectively divided the southern half of the proposed battleground into a series of zones that Morrison believed could be satisfactorily defended with the limited number of troops he had available.

Morrison's front line of pickets, consisting of three companies (estimated 150 all ranks) of the Lower Canada Voltigeur Regiment and the thirty Mohawk warriors, were stationed just outside and within the skirt of the woodlands on the northeast side of the open fields. Behind them, a detachment of around twelve Provincial Dragoons formed an extended picket line along the western edge of the east ravine. Approximately 200 yards (183 meters) further back, on the western side of the centre gully and immediately alongside the riverbank main road, the British right flank was composed of Lieutenant Colonel Pearson's Light Infantry command. This consisted of the two "flank" companies of the 49th Regiment (estimated 75 all ranks) and two companies of the Canadian Fencible Regiment (estimated 120 all ranks), both arranged in a stepped or "Echelon" formation. To their left and slightly to the rear, a second body of troops was made up of three companies of the 89th Regiment (Captain George Barnes) (estimated 155 all ranks), also in an echelon formation. Between these two infantry positions a single 6-pounder gun provided the immediate artillery support under Lieutenant Henry Kersteman (estimated 15 all ranks).

Around 700 yards (640 meters) to the left-rear of this front line, Morrison's main force of two 6-pounder guns (Captain Henry Jackson) (estimated 45 all ranks), eight companies of the 49th (Lieutenant Colonel Charles Plenderleath) (estimated 340 all ranks), and five of the 89th (Major Miller Clifford) (estimated 155 all ranks), were held at the British camp, with orders to assemble in parallel column formations should an alarm sound.

As dawn broke, the opposing picket lines began, either by accident or an overly alarmed sentry, a round of firing that quickly escalated into a skirmish, moving through the highly obstructed forest. The sounds of this firing were soon heard in the respective camps and prompted both sides to come to the alert and mobilize for action.

In the main British camp, interrupted in the midst of cooking their breakfast, the troops grabbed whatever sustenance they could and gobbled it down as they fell into their assigned regimental columns, with the 89th having its right hand company in front and the 49th its left. They then waited, and waited, for the expected American attack that the firing suggested was on its way. Instead, the firing eventually died down and no enemy appeared. However, the troops were kept in their columns and warned to be ready to move at a moment's notice.

At the American camp, General Boyd had assembled his column-of-march and had been obeying General Lewis' latest orders by commencing his downriver march, when an irate General Wilkinson countermanded the move and ordered Boyd to march his formation back to its starting point. They then stood around, in the face of a heavy downpour, waiting for someone to tell them what they were to do next.

Around 10:00 a.m. Captain Mulcaster's gunboats renewed their action against the American gunboat's at Cooks Point, precipitating a steady round of counter bombardment between the two detachments. This firing also echoed downriver, causing alarm and prompting a significant number of the unarmed transports to unilaterally cast off and either sail further downriver or cross to the American side of the river.

By noon the continuing chilling rain had saturated the waiting troops from both sides. Morrison realized that the Americans were not going to make the first move and could simply march away, losing him the temporary advantage of choosing his battleground. He therefore sent orders for his advance units (Voltigeurs and Natives) to advance through the woods and provoke an engagement with the American pickets.

For General Boyd, the interminable waiting had been punctuated by a succession of orders that arrived and then were almost immediately countermanded, exhausting what little patience he had left. Riding down to the riverbank opposite to where Willkinson's boat lay anchored offshore, Boyd mustered what little military deference remained toward his senior officer and bellowed across the open water. Although the exact phrasing of his subsequent words are (perhaps politely) not recorded with exactitude, the effect was that he would be grateful if the general were to rise from his bed and decide what he wanted his men to do.

Shortly thereafter, a message arrived from the senior general's boat that as word had arrived from General Brown that the way ahead was clear, the flotilla would sail and Boyd's force would march downriver without delay, while a detachment of artillery would be landed to support the rearguard in case of any minor skirmish. However, should the enemy make a more serious assault, Boyd was to take his command again and handle the enemy roughly in battle. Having finally received some

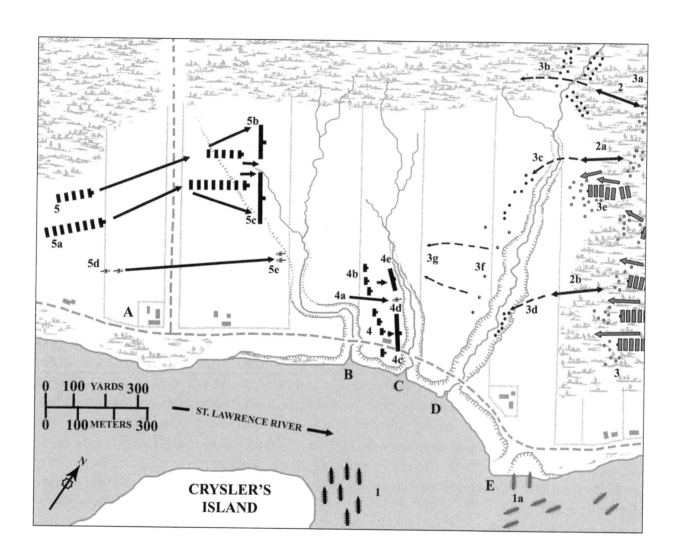

THE OPENING MOVES, AS THE BRITISH PROVOKE AN ENGAGEMENT

A   John Crysler's Farm
B   west gully
C   centre gully
D   east ravine
E   Cook's Point

9:00 a.m.–2:00 p.m.

1. Boats from the British "Corps of Observation" (1) sail downriver below Crysler's Island and engage the American line of picket boats (1a) stationed at Cook's Point (E). This action of manoeuvre and firing continues intermittently throughout the day, targeting both enemy vessels and any onshore troop formations that come within range.

2. Around noon the British picket line (Voltigeur Regiment and Native allies) (2, 2a, 2b) advance to engage American pickets, prompting a massive response by the main American force. The British picket retires to their original positions along the western edge of the forest.

3. The main American force (3, 3a) advance west in columns through the dense woods, lead by a strong force of Light infantry. This causes the northern detachments of Voltigeurs and Native allies (3b) to retire through the forest running along the northern side of the open fields. The centre detachments of Voltigeurs (3c) retire toward the British advance force (4-4b), while the southern detachments (3d) retire from the woodline and take up a firing position within the east ravine (D). Heading the American advance, the Twenty-First Regiment (3e) breaks out of the woodland in broken order and begins a heavy, but disordered, fire toward the retreating British pickets.

In response, the small detachment of Upper Canada Light Dragoons (3f) make a rapid withdrawal west (3g) and plays little or no further part in the action.

4. The British advance force : 2 companies, 49th Regiment and 2 companies Voltigeurs (4), 1x 6-pounder gun (4a), 3 companies 89th Regiment (4b), advance and form line along the western edge of the centre gully (C) (4c,4d,4e).

5. The British main force: 5 companies, 89th regiment (5) and 8 companies, 49th regiment (5a) advance from their encampment at Crysler's farm in column and then deploy into line (5b, 5c). The remaining two pieces of 6-pounder artillery (5d) advance and unlimber on top of a slight rise in the ground (5e) just west of the west gully (B).

definitive orders, Boyd directed his huge column to march east, only to hear the sounds of gunfire erupting in the west as the two lines of pickets once again began their engagement in the woods. Torn by his two sets of orders, Boyd again opted to turn back and fight, ordering his rearmost unit (the Fourth Brigade [Brigadier General Swartout]) to lead the way and move to the right. They were then followed in turn by the Third Brigade (Brigadier General Leonard Covington), which was to move to the left, and Boyd's own First Brigade (under the acting command of Colonel Isaac Coles) moving up into the centre. At the rear, cavalry detachments from the Second Dragoons (Major John Woodford) and two

AMERICAN UNITS ON THE FIELD AT CRYSLER'S FARM, NOVEMBER 11, 1813[*1]

Brigadier General Parker Boyd

First Brigade (Colonel Isaac Coles)
Twelfth Regiment (Major Robert Nicholas), est. 250–275 all ranks
Thirteenth Regiment (Colonel James Preston), est. 250–275 all ranks

Third Brigade (Brigadier General Leonard Covington)
Ninth Regiment (Lieutenant Colonel Thomas Aspinwall), est. 350–375 all ranks
Sixteenth Regiment (Colonel Cromwell Pearce), est. 250–275 all ranks
Twenty-Fifth Regiment (Colonel Edmund Gaines), est. 400–440 all ranks

Fourth Brigade (Brigadier General Robert Swartout)
Eleventh Regiment (Lieutenant Colonel Timothy Upham, absent with boat guard), est. 300–350 all ranks
Fourteenth Regiment (Lieutenant Colonel Timothy Dix), est. 280–300 all ranks
Twenty-First Regiment (Colonel Eleazer Ripley), est. 450–500 all ranks

Reserve "Boat Guard" (Lieutenant Colonel Timothy Upham)
Detachments from the First, Third, and Fourth brigades (est. 650–700 all ranks)

Cavalry

Second Light Dragoon Regiment (Major John Woodford), est. 125–170 all ranks

Artillery

Second Artillery Regiment (Lieutenant Henry Craig), est. 50–65 all ranks
Light Artillery Regiment (Lieutenant Armstrong Irvine), est. 20–30 all ranks
6 x 6-pounder field guns

6-pounder artillery pieces (Lieutenant Armstrong Irvine) completed the nearly 2,500 man force now advancing on the 200-strong Allied picket line. Morrison was about to get his wish — in spades![*1]

Back at the beach, the additional four American artillery pieces were still in the process of being landed, but only with much difficulty and a considerable delay, leaving Boyd devoid of this artillery support for some time to come. In addition, once the guns were eventually landed, it was realized that there were no available docile artillery-draft horses to pull them. The only horses that could be requisitioned to pull the heavy guns and limbers were some high-spirited cavalry mounts taken from the disgruntled Second Dragoons.

From the very start, Boyd's command ran into problems:

- The heavy undergrowth and fallen tree limbs disrupted any attempt to maintain a cohesive and coherent advance by the separate columns.
- The columns were under constant fire from the almost invisible Voltigeurs (in their grey uniforms) and experienced Mohawk warriors.
- The wet weather had rendered many of the men's loaded but unused muskets inert, as the ignition powder of the flintlocks had become saturated and required replacement before they would fire.
- Having been previously marched back and forth, a number of the units marching in the First Brigade's column had become "clubbed" or were in a reversed-order formation to that normally used, causing confusion in the ranks. This was compounded when some of the clubbed units attempted to rearrange themselves while advancing through the dense forest, which only made things worse and chaotic.

Engaging the British pickets, the Fourth Brigade's leading regiment, the Twenty-First, under the acting command of Major Joseph Grafton, backed by the Fourteenth and Eleventh regiments, soon pushed back the greatly outnumbered Voltigeurs and Mohawk Natives. But in the process they moved further and further to their right (north), thus increasing the separation between themselves and the still-disrupted First Brigade, which was still trying to sort itself out. On the left (south) flank, General Covington's Third Brigade was more cohesive and had an easier line of advance, as their stretch of woodland had been partially cleared and contained the riverbank road. Nonetheless, once the increased sounds of firing reverberated from the north, the previously restrained and pent-up enthusiasm of the men was released. Some units increased their pace, while others began cheering, disrupting the cohesion of the advance and making the passing of orders difficult in the resultant noise.

Reaching the edge of the woodlands, the right wing of the Voltigeurs raced across the open ground toward the east ravine. While close behind, the inertia of the Twenty-First's pursuit now worked against them, as the regiment burst from the woods in a disorganized state. In response, the small detachment of Provincial Dragoons also retired with haste back toward their main lines, where the patient British troops finally had a viable enemy target to engage.

Having assessed the sounds of firing coming from the woods, Lieutenant Colonel Pearson and Captain Barnes were well able to determine the location of the fighting and reacted accordingly by bringing up their retired echelon companies to "dress" on the leading company, thus forming their line-of-battle with their single artillery piece situated in the intervening gap. To the rear, Morrison advanced his two regiments and artillery some three hundred yards, where a slight rise in the ground gave the artillery the advantage of being able to fire at an elevated degree beyond Barnes' formation toward the approaching Americans. Meanwhile, on the eastern side of the battlefield, the columns of the American Third and First Brigades, as well as the following cavalry, also arrived and began forming their line-of-battle, all the while under long-range fire from the British artillery.

Nearest the river and on the roadway was the American left flank, composed of the Second Light Dragoon Regiment (Major Woodford). To their right, the three regiments of Brigadier General Covington's Third Brigade (sequentially the Sixteenth, Twenty-Fifth, and Ninth regiments), formed their line along the east side of the east ravine, while further to their right the still-disorganized First Brigade regiments (Twelfth and Thirteenth) almost broke and ran under the British artillery fire, but after an initial short retreat and a further delay, eventually also formed a rough line and moved back up to the lip of the east ravine.

To the right again, the Twenty-First Regiment, still in a disrupted column, was joined by its titular commanding officer, Colonel Eleazer Ripley, who had been absent from his unit when the order to march had been given. Behind and again to the right, the Fourteenth and Eleventh regiments

THE AMERICANS MOVE TO ATTACK THE BRITISH LEFT FLANK

B   west gully
C   centre gully
D   east ravine
E   Cook's Point

2:00 p.m.–3:00 p.m.

1. The main body of American troops arrives and deploys along the east side of the east ravine (D). The Third Brigade: Sixteenth (1), Twenty-Fifth (1a), and Ninth (1b) regiments form line. This forces the Voltigeur detachment (1c) in the ravine to retire on the British advance line (1d), while the centre detachment of Provincial Light Dragoons (1e) and Voltigeurs (1f) retire behind the line. The American First Brigade: Twelfth (1g) and Thirteenth (1h) regiments, having become "clubbed" in the initial march, remain disrupted when they come under long-range artillery fire from the British artillery (4b) and can only form a partially disordered line. The Fourth Brigade's Twenty-First Regiment (1i) remains disordered, while the other Fourth Brigade regiments, Eleventh (1j) and Fourteenth (1k), remain in column.

2. The Eleventh and Fourteenth regiments (1j, 1k) come under fire from detachments of the Lower Canadian Voltigeur Regiment and Native allies (2). Looking to initiate the American attack on the British left wing, the Eleventh and Fourteenth regiments are advanced (2a) and push back the British/Native Light troops (2b). Attached to the attack in support, the Twelfth and Thirteenth regiments are delayed by the necessity of reforming their column formations, then march to follow (2c, 2d) through the forest. The Twenty-First Regiment forms line and advances in the

open across the fields (2e), maintaining a position parallel to the sounds of the American advance within the forest.

3. Leading the attack, the Eleventh (3) and Fourteenth (3a) regiments push back the Voltigeur detachment (3b) and Native allies (3c) to a point alongside the British line's left flank. While the Natives remain under the cover of the woodlands, elements of the Voltigeurs break from the woods and run for the safety of the left wing of the 89th Regiment (4), hotly pursued by the American vanguard. Deeper in the woods, the Twelfth (3d) and Thirteenth (3e) regiments, make a slower, broken advance through the dense underbrush.

4. The main force of the 89th (4) and 49th (4a) regiments, supported by the two guns (4b), remain on the alert in the face of the visible advance of the Twenty-First Regiment (4e) and the sounds of firing from the woods.

5. The U.S. Second Light Dragoon Regiment (5) arrives on the field, and takes up a position astride the riverbank road on the east side of the east ravine (D).

completed the American formations on the field, but remained in column and still under harassing fire from the left wing of the Voltigeurs and Native pickets — who were now lining the edge of the swampland forest running along the north side of the battlefield.

Without any artillery to reply in kind at this longer range, General Boyd was left with little alternative but to close with the enemy and commence a musket-range engagement (i.e., at less than 150 yards [137 meters]). Because the ground on his left flank was obstructed by the intervening ravine/

111

gullies and was visibly defended by the British right flank, Boyd decided to make his initial attack on the British left flank by pushing the Fourteenth and Eleventh regiments through the forest to hit the 89th on its open left flank. At the same time, the Twenty-First were directed to form line and advance down the open field in parallel with the main columns inside the forest. To support this already sizeable force of around 800 men, Boyd added the First Brigade's Twelfth and Thirteenth complement of around 700 men as a reinforcement. This resulted in a total of around 1,500 men preparing to attack an estimated 250 men of the 89th regiment.

Being already in column, the Fourteenth and Eleventh stepped off without delay and quickly disappeared from sight into the forest, followed shortly thereafter by the renewed sounds of gunfire. In the field, however, the First Brigade regiments, having only just deployed into line, were delayed while they reformed their column before marching at the quick-step to catch up. Finally, the Twenty-First Regiment, having formed its own line, began its advance toward the enemy following the northern boundary of the open ground, However, this advance was also slowed by the need to clear a passage through the succession of split-rail fences that marked the field boundaries.

Using the sounds of gunfire from the woods as a guide to gauge the approach of the enemy, plus the visible position of the advancing Twenty-First Regiment, Morrison wheeled the 89th Regiment back, like a swinging door that was hinged on the right, creating a new "refused" alignment, eliminating the previously exposed left flank. He then completed this regiment's preparedness to meet the enemy at close range by ordering, "Fix Bayonets!"

Morrison's timing for this move was immaculate, as it had scarcely been completed when the first of the Voltigeurs broke out from the treeline and ran for the protective screen of redcoated infantry. Behind them, again hot-foot in pursuit, charged the leading body of the American Eleventh and Fourteenth regiments, only to be brought up short in their headlong chase by the intimidating sight of a solid line of disciplined enemy infantry, standing silently and directly in front.

Reacting to the new situation, the American regimental commanders began a desperate attempt to deploy their men into a similar line formation. However, the disruptive effect of the forest's passage while under hidden fire and the immediacy of the highly visible enemy caused many men to begin firing independently instead of taking their places in the line and commencing volleys. As a result, for a few moments the emerging American regiments were disorganized and vulnerable — all the opportunity Morrison and his disciplined men needed to do their job.

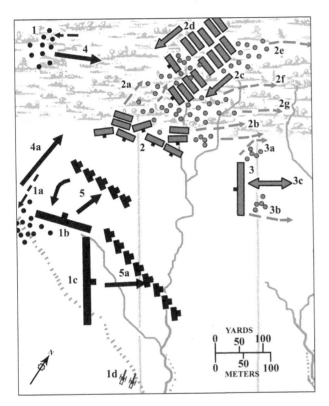

THE INITIAL AMERICAN ATTACK IS ROUTED.

3:00 p.m.–3:30 p.m.

1. Reacting to the sounds of firing by their Native allies (1) in the forest, and the arrival of the retreating Voltigeur detachment (1a), the 89th Regiment (1b) wheels backward on its right, securing the British left flank just before the American forces burst from the treeline. The 49th Regiment (1c) remains facing to the east while the artillery (1d), on the slight rise in ground, traverse their aim to target the advancing enemy.

2. The Eleventh and Fourteenth (2) regiments burst out from the forest in hot pursuit and in a mixed and disordered state. Seeing the 89th regimental line directly in front, many men begin firing independently, while others make a desperate attempt to form their own line-of-battle, but before this can be achieved the Americans are hit by devastating volleys of British firepower that bring the American attack to a halt. Under continued close-range British volley fire, the American position collapses and routs (2a, 2b). Fleeing back into the woods, the broken American regiments collide with the advancing Twelfth (2c) and Thirteenth (2d), precipitating a cascade collapse and rout of the entire initial American attack (2e, 2f, 2g).

3. The Twenty-First Regiment (3) advances to cover the American rout, but becomes disrupted when men from the line break ranks and take cover before firing (3a). Coming under fire from the 49th Regiment (1c), the Twenty-First Regiment, having used much of its ammunition in the initial phase of the battle, runs low on ammunition. Suffering additional casualties and desertions (3b) the regiment is forced to withdraw toward the east (3c).

4. With the rout of the Americans, the British Native allies (4) and Voltigeurs (4a) again advance and commence harassing the Americans within the forest.

5. Pressing their advantage and looking to sweep the broken Americans down the field, the 89th Regiment changes formation and marches in echelon of companies to the right (5), while the 49th Regiment advances in echelon of companies to the front (5a).

Opening up with a devastating pair of mass volleys, the 89th continued firing by company, putting a deadly fusilade of firepower into the already recoiling Americans. In addition, firing from their elevated position, the two rear British artillery pieces added their own shots to the mix. Unable to form a line and return fire, first the head and then the remainder of the Fourth Brigade's column disintegrated, as the men turned tail and broke. Unfortunately, as they fled they collided with the First Brigade regiments, just then emerging from the woods. Disintegrating into a confused mass of men moving in two opposite directions, the American attack collapsed on the spot.

Seeking to save the moment, Ripley brought forward his Twenty-First Regiment, intending to make a bold demonstration that would rally the broken American regiments and enable them to reform and renew the attack. Instead, some of the men in his line broke ranks and sought the cover of nearby trees from which to fire on the enemy at long range. The American attack had now completely stalled and it was Morrison's turn to move.

Changing his two regiments' formation from a solid line to line in echelon (i.e., "stepped"), Morrison advanced on the wavering Americans. Seeing a "wall" of disciplined troops, marching in silence with fixed bayonets and only stopping momentarily to pour in a volley of fire at an ever-decreasing range, proved to be too much for the Fourth and First brigades to cope with. As a result they routed, either down the open field or back into the forest, once again closely followed and harassed by the Voltigeurs and Natives. Downfield, the Twenty-First Regiment initially remained intact, apart from those who had chosen to go to ground. However, they were now seriously outmatched in both firepower and discipline. In addition, the excessive use of ammunition by individuals firing without orders had exhausted the ammunition supply. Seeing increasing numbers of men breaking out from the line and retreating, Ripley bowed to the inevitable and ordered the remainder of his regiment to retreat back to its starting point.

On the southeast side of the field, the American Third Brigade commander, Brigadier General Leonard Covington, watched the repulse occuring and decided to make his own attack on the British line. Had he moved simultaneous to the initial attack, there is little doubt that the American superiority in numbers and firepower would have carried the day. Instead, this American left flank assault was about to advance under the full focus of Morrison's attention and the fire of the British artillery.

Advancing in succession from left to right, the Sixteenth, Twenty-Fifth, and Ninth regiments

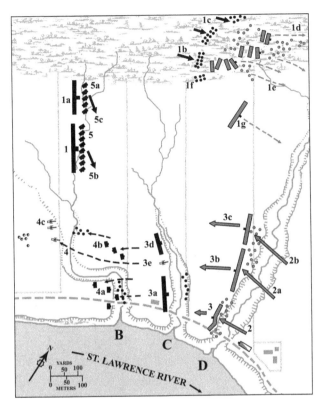

THE AMERICAN ATTACK ON THE BRITISH RIGHT FLANK (ADVANCE)

B   west gully
C   centre gully
D   east ravine
E   Cook's Point

3:15 p.m.–3:45 p.m.

1. With the initial threat of the Americans driven back, the 49th (1) and 89th (1a) regiments halt and form line, stabilizing the British left flank. In the forest, the northern detachment of the Lower Canada Voltigeurs (1b) and Native allies (1c) continue to press and harass the broken and retreating intermixed formations of the Eleventh, Twelfth, Thirteenth, and Fourteenth regiments (1d, 1e). At the woodline, smaller detachments of Voltigeurs and Native allies (1f) harass the retreat of the Twenty-First Regiment (1g).

2. As the American retreat on the right flank begins, the Third Brigade on the American left flank starts its advance to attack the British advance line. The Sixteenth Regiment (2), Twenty-Fifth Regiment (2a), and Ninth Regiment (2b) descend into the east ravine (D) and become disordered in the boggy and muddy defile.

3. Emerging from the east ravine (D), the Sixteenth Regiment (3) comes under a heavy fire from the advanced companies of the 49th Regiment and Voltigeurs (3a). Similarly, the Twenty-Fifth (3b) and Ninth (3c) regiments reform and then advance while under fire from the 89th advance companies, the associated Voltigeur picket detachment (3d), and the single British artillery piece (3e).

4. Under increasing threat of being outflanked on the left and greatly outnumbered, the British advance line is forced to retreat. Following the removal of the 6-pounder gun to a new position on the higher ground (4) the 49th/Voltigeur companies cross the west gully (B) and fall back (4a), but become partially disordered and lose men to the similarly advancing Sixteenth Regiment. The 89th companies and associated Voltigeurs retreat in good order (4b) toward the British guns (4c).

5. Observing the threat on the British right flank, Colonel Morrison changes the formation of the main companies of 49th (5) and 89th (5a) into echelon of companies and marches them diagonally across the field (5b, 5c) toward the advancing enemy formations.

began their disciplined march down the eastern side of the large east ravine. However, the combined effect of the rain-saturated embankment, the meandering rain-swollen creek, and adjacent boggy terrain disrupted the essential line discipline, causing men to slip, slide, and founder in the treacherous conditions. They then had to clamber up the equally treacherous western side, with saturated clothing and mud-encrusted boots, causing many more men to lose their footing and slide back down, further destroying each unit's integrity and cohesion. The result was that more of a mob of men than a line emerged onto the upper ground, only to find themselves looking down the barrels of the British force in front of them — less than two hundred yards (183 meters) away.

Not intimidated in the slightest by the numerical odds facing him, Lieutenant Colonel Pearson patiently waited while the bulk of the Sixteenth Regiment emerged and began desperately forming a line-of-battle before ordering his own line to fire. As a single unit, every musket in Pearson's line, accompanied by the adjacent 6-pounder cannon (Lieutenant Henry Kersteman), fired into the confused mass before them, scything down men left and right. Impressively, the Sixteenth did not break and run under this onslaught, but reformed their ranks and then began to reply — albeit in a slightly less disciplined kind.

To the Sixteenth's right, the Twenty-Fifth and Ninth regiments had also only crossed the east ravine with difficulty, but due to the easier terrain, they had reformed on the other side with greater speed and discipline. They then advanced, threatening to turn Captain Barnes' left flank and potentially cutting Pearson and Barnes off from their main line with their backs to the river. However, Colonel Pearson was too canny a soldier to let himself be trapped in this manner. Despite just having fallen from his horse when it was shot from under him, he ordered the entire British advance line to make an immediate fighting retreat to the western side of the west gully, thus closing the distance to the main British line. In a tightly run race, Pearson and Barnes' infantry detachments made their retreat, covering the removal of Kersteman's artillery piece before taking up new positions beyond the west gully; but in the process losing a number of wounded and stragglers to the American line that was pushing past the centre gully with equal speed. In addition, by reforming further back, Barnes' formations now partially masked (blocked the firing of) two of the three British artillery pieces.

On the British left flank, Morrison saw the growing threat to his right and, without any reserve, attempted to blunt the American advance by taking his already well-used 49th and 89th units diagonally across the battlefield in an echelon of

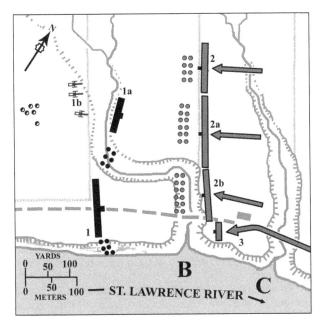

YARDS
0   50   100

0   50   100
METERS

B

── ST. LAWRENCE RIVER **C**

THE BRITISH AT BAY

B   west gully
C   centre gully

Approximately 3:30 p.m.

1. The advance companies of the 49th and Voltigeurs (1) establish a defensive position to the west of the west gully (B) and engage the approaching American line. After retreating, the advance companies of the 89th Regiment and associated Voltigeurs (1a) reform on the slight elevation, but mask (block) the firing of two of the three British artillery pieces (1b).

2. The American line: Ninth (2), Twenty-Fifth (2a), and Sixteenth (2b) regiments, covered by a forward screen of light troops, engages the British.

3. A small detachment of men returning from the rear (under Lieutenant R. Kirby) arrive and form on the left of the Sixteenth Regiment.

companies, bringing them directly down on the Third Division's right flank, while protecting his own left flank if the Americans appeared once more from the woods.

Arriving within firing range of the American line and seeing no sign of any threat from the northern forest, Morrison re-established his line-of-battle and engaged the Americans in the classic Napoleonic battlefield duel of firing volley after volley into the enemy formations at close range with the intent of making them break and run. In this circumstance the training and discipline of the British troops, coupled with a steadier and there-fore deadly, musket volley firepower, as well as each British soldier's larger ammunition cartridge boxes, gave them the edge, as casualties on both sides continued to mount and ammunition began to run low. Behind the British front line, although perhaps at a distance of over three hundred yards, the three British artillery pieces, their front now having been cleared, recommenced their own medium-range destructive work on the American formations,

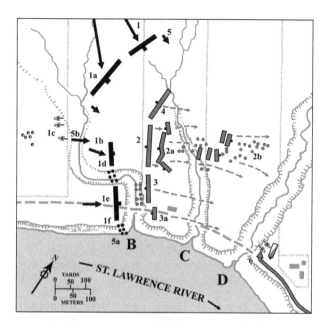

THE AMERICAN LINE BREAKS

B   west gully
C   centre gully
D   east ravine

3:30 p.m.–4:00 p.m.

1. With the arrival of the main body of the 89th (1) and 49th (1a) regiments on the British left flank, the American's are thrown onto the defensive. The advance companies of the 89th (1b) advance to the lower ground, clearing the front of the British artillery (1c), thus allowing the three guns to target the American line. On the British right flank the composite advance force of the 49th and Voltigeurs (1d,1e,1f) advance and secure the ground to the riverbank.

2. At the centre of the American line, the Twenty-Fifth Regiment (2) receives the heaviest part of the British fire. With ammunition running low, and taking increasing casualties, the regiment initially recoils and becomes disordered (2a) before breaking and routing (2b).

3. With the line breached in the centre, the Sixteenth Regiment (3) and Kirby's detachment (3a), also running out of ammunition, begin a withdrawal toward their initial position beyond the east ravine (D) to re-ammunition.

4. Left alone to contest the action, the Ninth Regiment (4) also begins a retreat to the east side of the east ravine (D).

5. As the Americans retreat the entire British line (5, 5a) begins to advance, while the single British advance gun (5b) is limbered up and follows the infantry's advance.

6. The first U.S. artillery (2 x 6-pounder) unit (6), having arrived on the field, takes up a firing position alongside the riverbank road on the east side of the east ravine (D) as the American infantry begins its retreat and begins firing on the advancing British line.

while the Americans still had nothing on the field at this point to match.

Placed relatively near the centre of the current American line, the Twenty-Fifth Regiment (Colonel Edmund Gaines) suffered a disproportionate number of casualties as it became the focus of the British infantry and artillery's firing. Eventually, running short on ammunition, parts of the regiment's line began to waver and then broke, abandoning the line and the field, splitting the American line in two. On the American left, nearest the river, Colonel Cromwell Pearce's Sixteenth Regiment was also rapidly running out of immediate ammunition and, seeing their right flank become exposed, Pearce ordered a withdrawal toward the eastern ravine. This only left the Ninth Regiment (Lieutenant Colonel Aspinwall) to maintain the field. Exposed, unsupported, under increasing enemy fire and running short on ammunition, the Ninth also retired. Fortunately, reinforcement now arrived for the Americans in the form of two 6-pounder artillery pieces (Lieutenant Armstrong Irvine). The two American guns immediately began firing from the riverbank toward Pearson's and Barnes infantry formations, both of which were advancing back toward their original positions at the centre gully. Shortly thereafter, the additional four American guns also arrived, under Lieutenant Henry Craig and Colonel Joseph Swift (U.S. Engineers). Seeing Boyd's remaining infantry units making efforts to re-ammunition and reform their battle lines near the eastern forest, and knowing that a strong reinforcement of infantry, derived from the boat guard and other detachments, was on its way under Lieutenant Colonel Timothy Upham, Swift recommended to Boyd that the newly arrived artillery be posted on the far (western) side of the east ravine as the centrepiece of a new line-of-battle. Agreeing to this plan, Boyd returned to his infantry. At the same time, Swift led the four artillery

pieces forward to their assigned positions. However, instead of crossing the east ravine by the relatively easier grade of the riverbank road, which was again within firing range of Colonel Pearson's advancing infantry, Colonel Swift led the artillery teams along the eastern rim of the east ravine and then had them cross in midfield, forcing them to pass through the rough and boggy obstacle only with great effort and difficulty. As each American gun finally came up the side of the ravine and was unlimbered, it was quickly brought into action against the nearest British unit that could be targeted, which happened to be the survivors of the eight companies of Lieutenant Colonel Plenderleath's 49th Regiment.

Seeing the 49th taking an increasing number of casualties from the American artillery, Morrison also noted that the enemy battery was still unsupported, as Boyd's reformed infantry units, including elements from the Fourth and First Brigades, had moved up to the brink but not re-crossed the ravine. There was therefore a momentary, if desperate, opportunity to charge the guns before their support arrived.

Sending his chief of staff, Lieutenant Colonel John Harvey, to Plenderleath with orders to make direct attack on the four guns with Major Clifford's five companies of the 89th in support.

Despite the obvious hazard of marching his men directly into the fire of a battery of undamaged

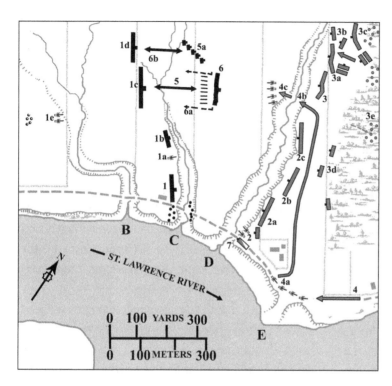

THE BRITISH ATTACK ON THE AMERICAN GUNS FAILS

B   west gully
C   centre gully
D   east ravine
E   Cook's Point

4:00 p.m.–4:30 p.m.

1. The British advance — 49th/Voltegeur regiments (1), 1 x 6-pounder (1a), 89th Regiment (1b) — returns to its initial defensive position on the west side of the centre gully (C), while the British left wing — 49th Regiment (1c), 89th

Regiment (1d) — secure the centre of the field. The British artillery (1e), on the rising ground to the rear, continues firing at long range on the reforming American line.

2. The two American 6-pounder guns (2) fire on the British formations, while the American line reforms and re-ammunitions. The Sixteenth (2a), Ninth (2b), and Twenty-First (2c) compose the American left wing.

3. Composite formations drawn from the previously routed Eleventh, Twelfth, and Fourteenth regiments (3, 3a, 3b) form the American right wing. Behind the line additional detachments either continue to reform (3c, 3d) or retreat through the forest (3e) toward the American flotilla.

4. Four artillery pieces (6-pounders) (4), arrive on the field, but are not immediately deployed (4a). Instead the decision is made to place the four guns at the centre of a new American line on the west side of the east ravine (D), supported by the advance of the entire line of infantry. The guns are therefore guided up the field (4b), but only cross the ravine with difficulty. Establishing their battery position (4c), they commence fire on the 49th Regiment (1c) but the American infantry line is not advanced in support, leaving the four guns unprotected and exposed.

5. Taking casualties from the artillery fire, the 49th Regiment advances to attack the guns (5), supported by the 89th marching in echelon of companies (5a). (*N.B.* evidence fails to confirm whether this was by the right or left.)

6. Suffering increasing casualties and becoming disordered by the firing and field fence obstacles, the charge of the 49th Regiment stalls and is eventually halted (6). While still under heavy fire, the regiment is safely withdrawn by having each company retire by files on the right (6a). The 89th also retire (6b), terminating the initial attack on the guns.

7. In response to the British attack toward the guns and the failure of the American line to cross the ravine, the Second Light Dragoon Regiment (7) begins to move across the east ravine (D) along the riverbank road to protect the guns.

artillery, Plenderleath followed his orders. Inevitably, while steady and impressive, the British advance also provided the American artillery with the widest possible target for the maximum amount of time. As a result, the 49th began to take crippling numbers of casualties and the advance began to falter. With no effective fire support from the two separate elements of the 89th on either side (Clifford on the left and Barnes on the right) Plenderleath recognized that his command would be destroyed if he continued to give the artillerists a prime target. He therefore contravened all the "textbook" instructions about not stopping a "charge" in mid-advance and did just that. Now he had the unenviable challenge of withdrawing those same already unsteady troops, in good order, through that same field of fire. If he simply ordered the line to "right about-face" it would leave the men marching with their backs to the enemy, while still presenting the same target — a recipe for an instant rout. Instead, he used a parade-ground manoeuvre that simultaneously withdrew the endangered companies, while presenting the smallest possible target to the enemy, by ordering each company to face to the right and then, with its right-hand files leading, marching away in a series of parallel mini-columns, two-men-wide, leaving the empty space of their company's line width between them.

Once the 49th had been withdrawn to what he considered a safer distance, Plenderleath halted his men, refaced them to their front, and dressed his companies before wheeling them around, thus reforming the exact line he had started with — whereupon he began firing back at the enemy guns. Not under the same devastating fire, the left division of the 89th had also withdrawn, maintaining its covering position on the flank of the 49th. Now, moving forward once again, it too opened fire; while on the right, Barnes brought forward his three companies to add to the cone of musketry targeting the American guns.

In short order, the American artillery found themselves in growing danger as the enemy once again advanced, while their own expected infantry support from the other side of the ravine failed to materialize. It became essential that the guns be withdrawn to safety back through the ravine. However, if the battery ceased fire in order to limber their guns and withdraw without infantry covering fire, there would be nothing to stop the British rushing forward, overrunning the position, and capturing the guns. Instead, Lieutenant Craig opted to withdraw three of the artillery pieces, covered by Lieutenant William Smith's single gun. As the American artillery fire faded, the British line made immediate preparations to advance once more.

Down on the riverbank road, Major John Woodford and his approximately 150 Second Dragoon cavalrymen had thus far been inactive in the battle, apart from acting as dispatch riders and supplying the horses now laboriously hauling the endangered cannon through the ravine. Seeing these guns being withdrawn without infantry support, Woodford received orders to advance and cover the artillery's retreat. Passing over the east ravine on the road, Woodford attempted to form his troopers up into a two-rank line, but was partially prevented from doing so by the increasingly accurate fire of Pearson's advancing detachments. Forced to act without delay to protect the guns retreat, and unable to target either Pearson's or Barnes' units due to the intervening centre gully, Woodford brought his ragged line of cavalry forward in an ever-accelerating wave toward the right flank of the now reformed 49th regiment. As the American cavalry passed directly across their front, each company of Pearson's infantry, Kersteman's 6-pounder gun, and then Barnes' formations had the perfect opportunity to pour in at

least one volley, inflicting increasing numbers of casualties on the already disorganized cavalry all along the way. However, once past this first British threat, Woodford's danger only increased as Barnes wheeled his left-hand company back, anchored on its right, thus presenting these troops with a perfect target of the American cavalry's backs. In a mirror image, Colonel Plenderleath reacted to the approaching mass of cavalry by calmly, but rapidly, wheeling his right-hand company of the 49th Regiment backward, creating yet another "refused" flank of muskets, all tipped with bayonets and pointed directly at the noses of the approaching horses. Together, the 49th and 89th companies opened up from the front and rear at a deadly close range, supported by additional firing from the British artillery to the rear. Under this onslaught, the already disorganized body of charging cavalry degenerated into a fleeing mass of horses and men. While the charge was stopped dead in its tracks and the American cavalry scattered back across the way they had come, repulsed and routed, it did achieve some sort of Pyrrhic victory, as the artillery were able to bring off their three limbered guns, but left the final gun, under Lieutenant William Smith, totally exposed as Barnes' men now rushed forward and quickly overran the position.

With nothing of any coherent American force remaining on the west side of the east ravine, Morrison seized the initiative provided by the

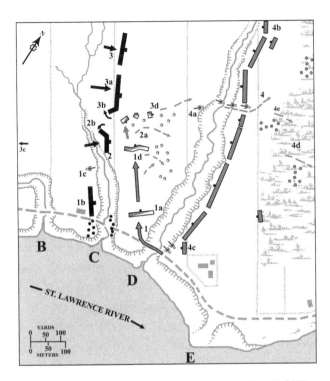

THE AMERICAN CAVALRY CHARGE IS REPULSED

B   west gully
C   centre gully
D   east ravine
E   Cook's Point

Approximately 4:30 p.m.

open target is the right flank of the main body of the reformed 49th Regiment (3a). Beginning their advance, the cavalry also comes under close-range fire from the 6-pounder gun (1c) resulting in additional casualties and some troops veering off (1d).

2. As the American cavalry pass close their front, the advance companies of the 89th Regiment (2) join in the firing, resulting in more losses to the charge (2a). The 89th then wheel back their left company (2b) allowing them to continue firing into the backs of the American cavalry.

3. Having reformed after the failed initial attack, the main body of the 89th (3) and 49th (3a) again advance, firing toward the guns, but are halted by the appearance of the American cavalry (1a). As the charge closes on their flank, the right company of the 49th Regiment wheels back to front the charge and puts in a volley at close range (3b). This, coupled with the mid-range fire of the British guns on the rise (3c, off map), and fire from the 89th (2b), routs the charge (3d).

4. Under cover of the cavalry charge, three of the four American guns (4) are limbered and withdrawn across the east ravine (D). However, one gun (Lieutenent W. Smith) (4a) is kept in action and is isolated from the main American line (4b, 4c) on the far side of the east ravine (D).

1. The Second Light Dragoons (1) cross the east ravine (D) and attempt to form a line in preparation for a charge, but are partially disrupted by fire from the companies of 49th/Voltigeurs (1b) in the advance line of British troops. Due to the broken ground, the nearest

capture of the American gun to bring up all of his infantry and form line along the ravine's lip, covered by the steady and continued fire support provided by his artillery.

The two armies now faced each other at a range of well under a hundred yards, separated only by the east ravine, and the scene was now set for a face-to-face pounding match, where only the determination to stand and fight would determine which side broke first.

After exchanging a number of volleys, it was the Americans who "blinked," as increasing numbers of individuals from each of the three partially reformed American brigades began to fall back in the face of the imminent volleys from the seemingly indestructible redcoats. Attempting to prevent a cascade of this disorder, Boyd made the decision to withdraw back to the edge of the woodlines. By this he sought to maximize the range for the British artillery, force the British infantry to become disrupted in their crossing of the ravine, and thus render them more vulnerable to any American fire. However, as each U.S. regiment and detachment made its move eastward the losses through desertion continued to mount, and some detachments simply decided not to stop at the edge of the wood, leaving the field entirely. Nonetheless, due to the initial American superiority of numbers there were still sufficient coherent units to make a determined stand, especially as the final reinforcements under Lieutenant Colonel Upham were literally only moments away from arriving. This stand never took place, however, as an order was seemingly delivered to Boyd to break off the action and retire on the boats. In the aftermath of the battle neither Wilkinson nor Lewis admitted to having issued such an order. Nor could Boyd recall who delivered it. Its effect, though, was immediate and decisive, as it was obeyed by each regiment and brigade commander without demur, and the entire American force marched away toward the treeline, assisted in its final retreat by a renewed barrage of long-range artillery fire from the British guns.

While there seemed to be nothing stopping Morrison from ordering a general advance with his remaining force, apart from the obvious fact that his men were in dire straits themselves, near to exhaustion and low on ammunition. The decision was taken away from him, when an entirely new American force began to appear along the riverbank road and adjoining woodline. This was Upham's reserve force of almost 600 entirely fresh troops, who advanced towards the east ravine and then began to form their own line-of-battle and appeared quite ready to continue the fight. Appearances could be deceiving, however, as this force's determination had been previously eroded by the sight of successively greater bodies of their fellow regimental companies retreating in differing degrees of disorder. This situation was not helped by the added factor of Upham being entirely unable to get any coherent direction or orders from any of the senior officers he encountered retreating from the field, with or without their regiments. Not even a meeting with Boyd elicited anything beyond an exhortation to "rush on." As

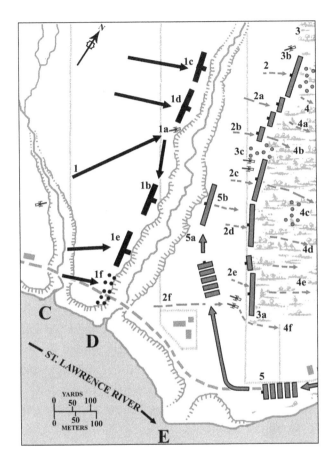

THE AMERICANS WITHDRAW

C   centre gully
D   east ravine
E   Cook's Point

4:30 p.m.–6:00 p.m.

1. With the dispersal of the American cavalry, the advance companies of the 89th Regiment (1) lead the renewed attack on the sole remaining American gun (1a). Overrunning the position, the 89th form line (1b) at the brink of the east ravine (D). In support, the remainder of the British line — 89th Regiment (1c), 49th Regiment (1d), 49th advance companies/ Voltigeurs (1e, 1f) — also advance to the western rim of the east ravine.

2. On the east side of the east ravine (D), the American line — composite companies of reformed Eleventh, Twelfth, and Fourteenth regiments (2, 2a, 2b), Twenty-First (2c), Ninth (2d), and Sixteenth (2e) and the two artillery pieces (2f) — initially make a stand but then retire to the treeline and begin to form a new defensive line.

3. The final American line (3, 3a) prepares to re-engage the British, but is subsequently ordered to withdraw to the American boats. (*N.B.* Due to lack of corroborative details, the participation and positions of the previously withdrawn three American artillery pieces (3b, 3c) in this formation are unconfirmed).

4. The American force retires through the forest, covered by a screen of light troops (4–4f).

5. American reinforcements (5), under Lieutenant Colonel Upham, arrive on the field. Upham's force advances to the centre of the field in order to conduct a rearguard action (5a) with the bulk of the British force but, significantly outnumbered and outgunned, his force suffers a number of casualties and is soon forced to retreat (5b).

a result, once on the battlefield, and after forming their seemingly formidable line-of-battle, Upham's units became the focused target of every British gun that was in range, and suffered accordingly. While the Americans replied in kind with volleys of their own, they knew with certainty that they were without any hope of additional support or reinforcements. Upham therefore faced the choice of seeing his command chewed to pieces in an ultimately futile defiant stand, or keeping his force intact and using it as a strong rearguard to deter the British from swooping down on the American beach while the already-retreating troops were in the process of re-embarking and highly vulnerable. Making the difficult decision to put duty before glory, Upham ordered his force to retreat back through the woods and act as the rearguard.

As the last of the American troops left the field, the heavens opened up with a downpour of rain, effectively signalling that no further firing of the weather-vulnerable muskets would be effective as disciplined volleys. Taking this as his cue, Morrison made the command decision to conserve what remained of his command for a future day's action and not attempt to push his troops through the woods against an enemy of unknown strength and dispositions. The Americans had certainly retreated, but were not necessarily defeated, and could use the obstructed wooded terrain to its greatest advantage

if he let them. He therefore advanced Colonel Pearson with a command composed of the flank companies of the 49th and Voltigeurs, to re-establish an advanced line of pickets within the woods and began the gruesome task of searching the battlefield for the wounded, dying, and dead.

At the American landing ground a sense of urgency, bordering on desperation, gripped many of the troops. This was especially true of the boat crews who, irrespective of their duties to remain and ferry their charges downriver, chose instead to make their own escape, leaving many of the exhausted infantry that had not already boarded with no option but to march downriver toward General Brown's advance guard at Cornwall. By nightfall, the American army was effectively split in two, with half their force being landed on the American side of the river and the remainder stuck on the northern bank, attempting to get out of striking range of what was believed to be a still-pursuing British force.

During the following few days, the previously vaunted, and delayed, campaign against Montreal collapsed surprisingly quickly. The American forces initially moved downriver through the Long Sault rapids. Whereupon Wilkinson held yet another council of his senior officers, and after a raucous and divided meeting the majority concurred with his recommendation that the campaign should be abandoned and the army should find a defendable winter encampment location. For the next two days Wilkinson's army maintained a shrinking bridgehead as they abandoned the northern shore to cross over to the American bank. During this time they were under constant British observation, but no attempt was made to initiate an attack, as the weakened forces available to Morrison could not have hoped to win a second time had the Americans fielded their remaining forces. The Americans then made an undignified and chaotic retreat up the adjacent Salmon River to the small community of French Mills. Here they began the laborious job of building themselves a fortified encampment with little proper equipment or tools, and with only a few days of rations immediately on hand. Nor did the weather cooperate, as a succession of days of freezing rain and frigid nighttime temperatures combined to turn the ground into a bog covered by a thin skin of frozen mud. The boats of the flotilla were either burned or scuttled in the river to impede any pursuit and prevent their capture, while many of the officers of the various corps, including Wilkinson and Boyd, found convenient excuses to claim leave or pressing duties elsewhere, thus effectively abandoning their men entirely.

In the aftermath of the action, the official reports penned by Generals Boyd and Wilkinson were artistic masterpieces of "spin," generating, in Boyd's case, the impression that the action had been virtually a victory for the American cause, only blunted, but not foiled, by the capricious hand of misfortune and luck. Wilkinson, on the other hand, chose to explain the failure of the battle by using the familiar technique of under-quoting his own participant troop numbers and subsequent casualties, while inflating those of the enemy, to a degree where the numbers of troops fielded by Morrison outnumbered those that Boyd brought to the field. To do this he not only doubled the numbers for those enemy units actually involved, but included at least three regiments that weren't even there! Similarly, to shift the odium of seeing the campaign collapse, Wilkinson also had the good fortune of having a ready-made scapegoat upon whom much of the blame could be foisted in the person of General Hampton, whom Wilkinson accused of deliberately sabotaging the success of the campaign by his incompetent leadership before and after Châteauguay and his defiant refusal to link up with Wilkinson's valiant forces. In turn, Hampton not only replied to these accusations with his own bluster of self-justification for his orders to withdraw, but passed the buck back to Wilkinson for failing to start his campaign on time and not reaching anywhere near where Hampton could meet him in the time allotted and restricted by his own army's lack of supplies. This round of recriminations and counter-accusations continued unabated during the following weeks, with vitriolic and accusatory letters being published by both officers and their respective supporters. Eventually, this mutually assured destruction drew in the entire spectrum of military and political hierarchy in Washington and laid the foundation for the subsequent Congressional inquiry that investigated the repeated American failures to fulfill their war aims.

Meanwhile, back in Upper Canada, Lieutenant Colonel Morrison maintained a watchful eye on the retreating American army, following it by having his own flotilla of boats shoot the Long Sault rapids on November 15th, allowing his reduced force to be linked up with reinforcement detachments at Cornwall. He then began a series of probes and secret reconnaissance incursions into the American positions at French Mills, leading him to the conclusion that the current chaos of the American positions rendered them highly vulnerable to a rapid strike — *if* Prevost immediately sent additional reinforcements to his aid. This recommendation was forwarded to Prevost, but to Morrison's frustration and chagrin Prevost not only vetoed this operation, he instructed Morrison to effectively disband his force by having the boats pulled up on shore at Cornwall and stored there for the winter. The troops that had come down from

ESTIMATE OF CASUALTIES, CRYSLER'S FARM, NOVEMBER 11, 1813[2]

N.B. American casualty rosters for this action are contradictory at best, caused either by honest error, the disruption of the American army following the battle, or the deliberate misrepresentation of figures in subsequent reports; thus leaving only general estimates possible.

British/Canadian
Killed:	est. 20–25 all ranks
Wounded:	est. 140–150 all ranks
Missing/Prisoner:	est. 9 all ranks

Native Allies
Wounded:	est. 1 warrior
Missing/Prisoner:	est. 3 warriors

American
Killed:	est. 100–200 all ranks
Wounded:	est. 230–275 all ranks
Missing/Prisoner:	est. 75–200 all ranks

Prescott and Kingston were then expected to march back the respective 80 and 140 miles (129 and 225 kilometers) to their bases, before going into their own winter quarters. As a sop to Morrison personally, Prevost also directed the victorious commander to travel down to the Lower Province and then cross over to England, there to deliver the news of his victory in person to Whitehall.[2]

CHAPTER 12

A New Broom

With the threat to Montreal eliminated and the lifeline to Upper Canada by way of the St. Lawrence River secure, Sir George Prevost, already displeased with his subordinates in Upper Canada, took the opportunity to reorganize that command by reassigning Major General Vincent to the garrison at Kingston and Major General de Rottenburg to Montreal. Major General Proctor, on the other hand, was peremptorily directed to return to Quebec to face what turned out to be a pre-determined military inquiry over his own defeats suffered on the Detroit frontier and implications of his degree of blame for Barclay's naval defeat — a rigged judicial crucifixion that had been established by Sir George Prevost for the sole purpose of deflecting onto Proctor any of his own culpability in creating the inevitable defeats, effectively ending Proctor's career and black-washing his name in future history books.

To replace Proctor, Prevost chose Lieutenant General Gordon Drummond and Major General Phineas Riall to lead the New Year's campaign in Upper Canada. Arriving at York, General Drummond paused to officially assume command as administrator of Upper Canada and commander of the troops on December 13, 1813, before immediately pressing on to personally assess the state of defences and troop deployments along the Niagara frontier. Learning of the American depredations at Newark, Drummond immediately ordered a retaliatory strike on the centre of American operations, Fort Niagara.

Although Colonel John Murray, the acting senior commander, had already commenced

Archives of Ontario, Acc. 693127.

Lieutenant General Gordon Drummond. G.T. Berthon, artist, circa 1882.

preparations for an assault on Fort Niagara immediately after occupying Fort George, the necessity of placing his troops and the destitute refugees under adequate cover in the face of bitterly cold weather had otherwise preoccupied his attention. In addition, the retreating Americans had taken or destroyed every boat on the west bank of the river leaving no immediately available means of transportation. Determined to exact revenge on the Americans for the mistreatment of their families and friends, the men of the Lincoln and Incorporated militias volunteered to collect and transport sufficient bateaux from the depot at Burlington Heights to allow the attack to take place. In bad weather and freezing temperatures, parties from the two militias, under the supervision of Captain Kerby (Incorporated Militia), brought the boats along the Lake Ontario shore to Four Mile Creek. To avoid detection, the boats were then hauled up onto the shore and manhandled across several miles of frozen countryside before being secretly relaunched into the Niagara River, well above Fort Niagara and its outlying batteries. The stage was now set for the war to move to the other side of the river.

For his part, General McClure had used the time following his retreat to his own shores to call out another draft of militia. He also placed Captain Leonard (First Artillery Regiment) in charge of Fort Niagara with a garrison of nearly 400 troops and issued a brave-sounding letter to Governor Tompkins, stating: "The enemy is much exasperated and will make a descent on this frontier if possible,

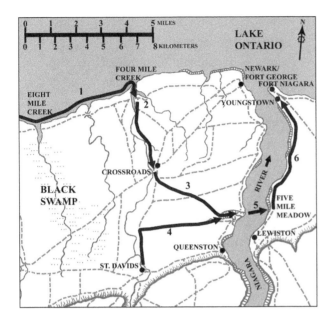

THE ROUTES TAKEN BY THE BRITISH TO ATTACK FORT NIAGARA, DECEMBER 17–19, 1813

1. The boats are sailed up from Burlington Heights (1).

2. The boats are hauled on shore at Four Mile Creek (2).

3. The boats are hauled overland to the Niagara River (3).

4. The British attack force marches from St. Davids (4) to rendezvous with the boats.

5. The crossing of the Niagara River (5).

6. The British column advances on Youngstown and Fort Niagara (6).

but I shall watch them close until a reinforcement of militia and volunteers arrive, when I shall endeavour to repossess myself of Fort George and drive them back to Burlington,"[1] before packing his bags and removing himself and his headquarters to the relatively distant safety of Buffalo.

THE ASSAULT ON FORT NIAGARA, DECEMBER 18/19, 1813

Meanwhile, having gained intelligence of the American positions and guard rotations, Lieutenant Colonel Hamilton (100th Regiment) was able to provide the British attacking force with a significant advantage for their planned attack on Fort Niagara. The night of December 17/18 was initially fixed for the attack, but bad weather and delays in logistics caused its postponement to the following night. However, despite every precaution warnings reached the Americans, resulting in the garrison at Fort Niagara being fully under arms throughout the nights of December 16/17 and 17/18. Some twenty-seven pieces of artillery were fully charged in the various bastions around the fort, and a stockpile of hand grenades was placed in each of the main buildings. But after two nights of being on the alert, and with no sign of any British movement, Captain Leonard inexplicably relaxed his guard and placed

AMERICAN GARRISON, FORT NIAGARA, DECEMBER 18/19, 1813[*2]

(Captain Leonard)
First Artillery Regiment, est. 17 gunners
Nineteenth Regiment, est. 50 all ranks
Twenty-Fourth Regiment, est. 60 all ranks
Detachments of around 200 recruits and convalescents from several unspecified regiments
Sick and invalids, 45 all ranks
Plus officers, artillerists, stores, and hospital staff, etc.

Estimated total: 400–450 all ranks

the garrison on a lower footing of readiness, while he rode out to visit his family at a farmhouse a few miles distant from the fort.[*2]

At St. Davids, Colonel Murray had gathered together his assault force of around 500 regulars and detachments of militia and Native warriors. Strict instructions had been issued that the attack was to be made with all muskets unloaded and that

> The troops must preserve the profoundest silence and the strictest discipline. They must on no account be suffered to load without the orders of their officers. It should be impressed on the mind of every man that the bayonet is

the weapon on which the success of the attack must depend.[3]

> — Lieutenant Colonel J. Harvey to Colonel Murray, December 17, 1813

There was also a concern that the Native allies might seek plunder or assault civilian women and children, which led to the express directive of General Drummond that no such activities would be tolerated. "I cannot consent to employ them except on this condition."[4]

Around midnight, the first half of the assault force embarked and pushed out into the frigid water. Manoeuvring to avoid large ice floes floating downstream, the men of the militias piloted the boats to the far bank. After an undetected landing had been made in a meadow about three miles (5 kilometers) above the fort, the advance party of about twenty men from the Grenadier company of the 100th Regiment and a team of gunners from the Royal Artillery moved off into the darkness. Behind them the remainder of the first wave secured the landing ground, and the boats returned to the Canadian shore to bring over the second wave. Maintaining total silence, the advance party reached the position of the first American picket, a tavern in the village of Youngstown about a mile (1.6 kilometers) from the fort. To their surprise they found the sentries indoors, sheltering from the intense cold, while the

Library and Archives Canada, C-18775.

(Above): *Fort Niagara,* S. Stretton, artist, circa 1806. Fort Niagara as seen from Lake Ontario prior to the war.
(Below): A similar view in winter (2011) as seen from Fort Mississauga on the Canadian side of the Niagara River.

remainder of the guard were sleeping or playing cards. The house was quickly surrounded and, on a signal, the British burst in on the negligent guards, putting every man to death at the point of the bayonet. In a similar manner, a second picket nearer to the fort was overrun and forced to reveal the night's password, without any warning being given to the unsuspecting garrison. By 4:00 a.m. the main force had arrived and divided into three columns, each with a specific target of attack.[5]

As the first column silently approached the ditches of the fort, it caught the American guards in the act of changing sentries at the exterior palisade gate and the small interior riverside gate wide open.

Fort Niagara in winter (2012) as viewed from across the Niagara River. Note the extensive volume of ice in the river (centre) and out on Lake Ontario (left).

Seizing the moment, Sergeant Spearman (100th Regiment) marched boldly up to the sentry and gave the appropriate password. Under cover of darkness and both soldiers being dressed in the standard long greatcoat common to both armies, the guard was momentarily lulled into accepting the newcomer as a fellow American soldier, an error that cost him his life. The way into the fort was now open and the sergeant forced his way into the fort's compound, followed by the remainder of that column, advancing at a run. Elated, the men raised a loud cheer, which unfortunately alerted the American garrison to the attack. For the next half hour a desperate hand-to-hand fight ensued, as each side sought to control the various buildings in the fort. Eventually,

FACING: CURRENT (2012) VIEWS OF THE HISTORIC SITE OF FORT NIAGARA.

(1) Looking north across the Niagara River from Fort George, clearly shows the vulnerability of Fort Niagara's original main entrance in the "south" redoubt. Positions marked refer to details in the 1814 plan of the fort (below).

(2) Blocked up throughout the War of 1812–1815, the restored and reopened "south" stone redoubt gatehouse (C) dominates the parade square with clear lines of fire from its upper gun deck and today again acts as the main entrance to the site.

(3) The "north" stone redoubt building (B).

(4) The "French Castle" and adjacent bake house/kitchen (A).

An 1814 map of Fort Niagara, appearing essentially as it did on the night the British attacked. Defensive positions and the routes of the British columns are highlighted.

A. The "French Castle"
B. The "north" stone redoubt
C. The "south" stone redoubt
D. The 1812–15 riverside gate into the fort
E. The "first" British column forces an entry through the exterior guardpost gate, allowing them to rush the riverside gate and gain entry to the fort proper
F. The "second" British column attacks the "salient point" of the south bastion
G. The "third" British column attacks the fort by scaling the eastern demi-bastion

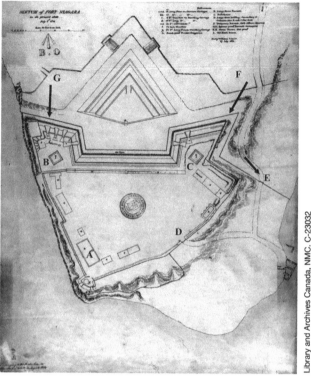

Library and Archives Canada, NMC. C-23032

ESTIMATE OF CASUALTIES, ASSAULT ON FORT NIAGARA, DECEMBER 18/19, 1813[6]

British
Killed: 1 officer, 5 rank and file
Wounded: 2 officers, 3 rank and file

American
Killed: 65 rank and file
Wounded: 2 officers, 12 rank and file
Prisoners: 14 officers, 12 sergeants, 318 rank and file

the garrison fell and the defeated Americans were herded into the parade square. At the same time, British detachments scoured the buildings looking for stragglers who might ignite the large supplies of ammunition in each structure, destroying the valuable prize they had won at such a slight cost. Only a handful of Americans escaped capture by dropping from the walls of the fort into the snow-filled ditches and crawling away into the night.[6]

BRITISH FORCE, ASSAULT ON FORT NIAGARA, DECEMBER 18/19, 1813[*5]

First Column (Targeting the main gate)
Forlorn Hope, 100th Regiment (Lieutenant Dawson), 20 rank and file
100th Regiment (Captain Fawcett) Grenadier Company, 40 rank and file
Royal Artillery (Lieutenant Charlton), 12 gunners
100th Regiment (Lieutenant Colonel Hamilton), five companies, 175 rank and file

**Second Column
(Targeting the salient point of the south bastion)**
1st (Royal Scots) Regiment (Captain Bailey) Grenadier Company, 90 rank and file

**Third Column
(Targeting the eastern demi-bastion)**
100th Regiment (Captain Martin), three companies, 135 rank and file

Reserve
41st Regiment (Lieutenant Bullock) Flank Companies, 88 rank and file

Total estimated force: 20 officers, 560 rank and file

Angel Art Ltd. Courtesy Old Fort Niagara Association, Inc.

The huge size of the now heavily stained garrison flag that flew over Fort Niagara in December 1813 can be gauged by the people alongside. Captured by the British, it was returned to U.S. hands in 1994 and is now on display at the Fort Niagara Historic site.

At dawn, General Drummond crossed the river and entered Fort Niagara. Awaiting him were the men of the victorious assault force and those Canadians and Natives who had been seized and incarcerated in the cells by McClure. Also waiting was a dejected Captain Leonard, who had returned to his fort only to find it captured. An inventory of the supplies in the fort revealed a wealth of items, including twenty-seven artillery pieces, 3,000 sets of muskets and bayonets, dozens of rifles, thousands of sets of leather accoutrements and cartridge boxes, camp equipment, medical supplies, and barrels of food and drink. Not to mention vast numbers of vitally needed shoes, trousers, shirts, and other clothing of every description, which were eagerly donned by the victorious but threadbare British and Canadian soldiers.

CHAPTER 13

Flames Along the Border: The Niagara Frontier, December 1813

At dawn on December 19, 1813, General Riall crossed the Niagara River with a force of some 1,000 regulars from the 1st (Royal Scots) (Lieutenant Colonel Gordon) and 41st Regiments (Major Richard Frend), as well as almost 500 Native allies. Landing just below the village of Lewiston, they marched upon the artillery batteries situated there. Facing this large force were a mere 127 officers and men of the New York State Militia (Major Bennett) and about fifty Tuscarora Native warriors. In an attempt to hold back the enemy long enough for support to arrive from Fort Schlosser, Bennett opened fire, but was soon outflanked and overrun, losing two cannon, seventeen men killed, an unnamed number of prisoners, and over 200 barrels of provisions and flour.[1]

With no significant opposition remaining below the escarpment, both sides of the river were now firmly in British hands. Regrettably, in retaliation for McClure's actions at Newark, numerous buildings at Youngstown and Lewiston were torched by both the British regulars and Canadian militia — a move that the Natives took as releasing them from their own injunction to restrain their actions. Pressing on into the countryside, the British Native allies destroyed the abandoned Tuscarora community before extending their looting and burning to nearby white homesteads and farms. At first little was done by the British, until they saw that women and children were also being targeted for the wrath of the warriors. Drawing the line, the British regulars sought to stop the attacks, to the point of fighting with their supposed allies.

Records indicate some twenty-seven American women and children were saved in this manner, at the cost of several wounded and one man killed amongst the British soldiers.

In another example of these soldiers' bravery, because part of the Fort Niagara garrison included some of the wives and children of the soldiers who were captured and would otherwise be left destitute and starving, special allowance was made to transfer these dependants to the Canadian side of the river to follow their spouses into captivity or parole. With ice floes crowding the river, however, crossing could prove to be a hazardous undertaking in the available small open boats. In one such case, a boat crewed by men of the 100th Regiment to transfer a young mother and her child was caught in the strong river current and, despite desperate efforts to catch ropes thrown from the shore, were swept out into Lake Ontario. Fortunately, a strong onshore northerly wind kept the boat within sight of land. As the temperatures plummeted that night, the surrounding ice floes froze together, trapping the boat over a half mile offshore but preventing a rescue boat from reaching them. With their rescuers unable to help until dawn, the senior NCO in charge of the boat, Sergeant Black, ordered his six men to lie down with the woman and child sandwiched in between them, covered as much as possible by their greatcoats and warmed by their body heat. The following morning a rescue boat was able to break its way through. Fully expecting the stranded crew and passengers to have frozen to death in the sub-zero temperatures, they were elated to find all alive and relatively unharmed.[2]

By December 21st, General Riall's column had razed Fort Schlosser and advanced within ten miles (16 kilometers) of Buffalo before retiring to Fort Niagara. The bulk of the assault force was now withdrawn to the Canadian side of the river, while a strong detachment of some 500 men was retained to garrison Fort Niagara. Despite seeing a large body of the enemy on his country's soil, General McClure failed to launch a counterattack. Instead he moved his headquarters further inland and handed over authority at Buffalo to Brigadier General Hopkins. He then issued public letters of complaint against the various State militias, blaming them for his plight and condemning his own subordinates for undermining his authority. In response, on December 20th General Hopkins wrote to Governor Tompkins, "I have to represent that the men of my brigade are unwilling to come under the command of General McClure.... His conduct since he has been out of the lines has disgusted the greater part of the men under his command and they have no confidence in him."[3]

While a prominent local citizen and militia officer wrote to the Governor in even stronger terms:

> In Buffalo, nothing but disorder and confusion prevails…. My opinion of General McClure … has convinced me that he is wholly incompetent to the command of this frontier during such times as the present. At all events, you may rest assured that he is universally detested by all the inhabitants; that his soldiers have no confidence in him, and his officers unanimously concur in the opinion of his unfitness to command…. Under these circumstances it will not be difficult for you to judge of the efficiency of any force under his command.[4]
>
> — John C. Spencer to New York Governor Tompkins, December 26, 1813

The only war that General McClure waged at this time was one of words with General Drummond. This took the form of a series of letters that were sent between the two commanders, whereby each accused the other of starting the sequence of depredations that had laid waste to both sides of the Niagara River during the previous weeks. Eventually, after hearing of McClure's attempts to implicate himself as the originator of approval for the razing of Newark, Secretary of War Armstrong sent an immediate refutation to New York State Governor Tompkins:

> … the abandonment of Fort George and burning of Niagara … were bad enough, but what shall we say of the surprise of Fort Niagara…. McClure had not, (as you seem to suppose) authority for doing anything he did. If he could not hold Fort George destroy it, but then let him take care of his principal fortress…. But away he runs to Buffalo…. He hints that Newark was burnt by my orders. This is a great error. My orders were to burn it if necessary to the defence of Fort George, not otherwise. But he does not defend Fort George, then burns Newark…. Relieve this man.[5]
>
> — December 26, 1813

Upon receipt of this directive, Governor Tompkins quickly relieved McClure of his command and replaced him with Major General Amos Hall, the regional militia commander.

Arriving at Buffalo on December 26, 1813, General Hall found the military situation in chaos. Some of the regular officers who were still loyal to McClure were openly expressing the view

POSITIONS ALONG THE NIAGARA RIVER, DECEMBER 1813

American

A. The "Creek" (Morgan's) battery
B. The navy yard slipways, warehouses, and barracks
C. Scajaquada Creek blockhouse and barracks
D. The "Sailor's" battery
E. Fieldwork battery
F. "Swift's" battery
G. Brigadier General Porter's house
H. "Dudley's" battery
I. "Fort Tompkins"
J. "Old Sow" battery
K. "Upper" river battery

British

L. "No. 2" river battery
M. Fieldwork battery
N. The "Red House" battery
O. The "Ferry" battery
P. "No. 1" river battery

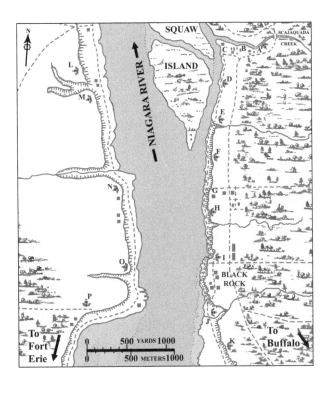

that because many of the citizens of Buffalo had opposed McClure, they were unworthy of protection and deserved to come under the hands of the enemy. Nevertheless, Hall took charge and began to sort out the mess. He even proposed putting together a new force to retake Fort Niagara or cross at Fort Erie in order to force the British to withdraw from Fort Niagara to defend their own frontier. Unfortunately, he was not to be given any time to remedy his precarious situation, as Generals Drummond and Riall were once again about to take the initiative in this winter war on the Niagara.

CHAPTER 14

Cold Steel and Hot Fire

Learning of the fall of McClure and the apparent chaos of the American command at Buffalo, Generals Drummond and Riall decided to make a pre-emptive strike on Buffalo as soon as possible. However, no boats were available at Fort Erie. Drummond therefore ordered that the large bateaux, used in the Fort Niagara crossing on the 19th, be hauled up the escarpment, portaged across country to Chippawa, and then brought up to Fort Erie in preparation for the assault. After considerable difficulties, the men of the Incorporated and Lincoln militias again succeeded in bringing the boats forward by the 26th and plans were made for the foray the following night. However, the appearance of American troops at the proposed landing site below Black Rock, plus the arrival of over 250 exhausted reinforcements from the 8th (King's) and 89th regiments, persuaded Riall to delay the attack for twenty-four hours. Instead, scouting parties slipped across in the darkness to reconnoitre the American positions and carry off prisoners for interrogation, causing an increased level of alarm amongst the American troops stationed along the riverbank.

On December 28th, General Drummond issued a general order to his troops and their Native allies on their duties for the attack and calling for his men to "never throw away their fire," but to rely on the bayonet "the weapon most formidable in the hands of British soldiers."[1] He also made an unequivocal and stern warning that the excesses of the post-Fort Niagara incident would not be tolerated on this occasion.

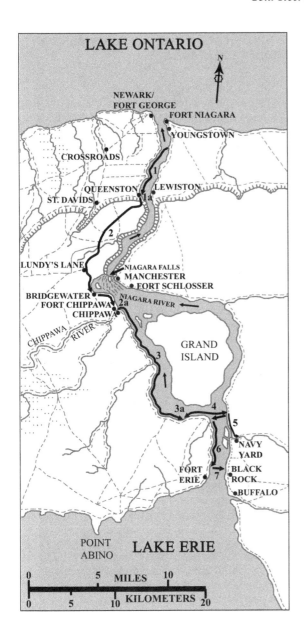

THE ROUTE FOLLOWED BY THE BRITISH BOATS IN PREPARATION FOR THE ASSAULT ON BLACK ROCK AND BUFFALO, DECEMBER 26–30, 1813

1. The boats are sailed up the Niagara River to Queenston (1) and hauled out of the water (1a).

2. The boats are hauled overland (2) to the Chippawa River and relaunched (2a).

3. The boats are sailed upriver to the first embarkation point (3a).

4. The first crossings and infantry landings (4) are made downriver from the U.S. navy yard.

5. The landed infantry advance to attack the navy yard positions and Black Rock (5).

6. The boats are moved up to the second embarkation point (6).

7. The second crossings and infantry landings are made from Fort Erie on Black Rock (7).

The plan of attack was for a two-pronged assault.[*2] In the first wave, General Riall, leading a strong body of regulars, militia, and Native allies, would land below Black Rock and capture the outlying American positions. The boats were then to return and bring over two additional waves of troops before moving upriver to Fort Erie to embark the fourth and final wave for their attack directly toward Black Rock under the cover of darkness and the main body of troops attacking along the riverbank.

BRITISH ORDER OF ATTACK, BLACK ROCK–BUFFALO, DECEMBER 29, 1813[2]

First Wave (Lieutenant Colonel Ogilvie)
8th (King's) Regiment, est. 240 rank and file
89th Regiment, Light Company, 55 rank and file
Militia volunteers, 25 rank and file
Native allies, detachment*

Second Wave (Major Frend)
41st Regiment, 250 rank and file
100th Regiment (Capt Fawcett) Grenadier
    Company, 50 rank and file
Militia Volunteers, 25 rank and file
Native allies, detachment*

Third Wave
Native Allies, detachment*

Fourth Wave (Lieutenant Colonel Gordon) directly on Black Rock
1st (Royal Scots) Regiment, 370 rank and file
Militia Volunteers (Major Simons) and remaining
    detachments of Native allies, detachment*
*Estimated composite of all four Native detachments,
    400 warriors

Meanwhile, on the other side of the river, General Hall had brought some semblance of order to the American forces in Buffalo. His main fixed artillery batteries between Buffalo and Black Rock were well situated atop a steep bank paralleling the river and

THE BRITISH ATTACK AND INITIAL AMERICAN DEFENSIVE SETBACKS

A. The "Creek" (Morgan's) battery
B. The navy yard slipways, warehouses, and barracks
C. Scajaquada Creek blockhouse and barracks
D. The "Sailor's" battery
E. Fieldwork battery
F. "Swift's" battery
G. Brigadier General Porter's house
H. "Dudley's" battery

1. The initial wave of British troops are ferried across the Niagara River and land undetected some distance below (off map) the Scajaquada Creek. The leading element of the British advance (Light Company, 89th Regiment) advance along the riverbank road (1), drive off the outlying American pickets (1a) at the Scajaquada Creek bridge, before rushing and overwhelming the "Creek" battery (A), the navy yard (B), the creek mouth blockhouse and barracks (C), and "Sailor's" battery (D). They are then forced to halt and wait, losing the impetus of the attack, while the remainder of the following waves of reinforcement troops (1b) arrive and take up the main advance. On the British left flank, the Native allies (1c) infiltrate through the forest.

2. The first American militia unit, the Erie County Militia (2), arrives from Buffalo and, in the darkness, run directly into the British line (2a) and is repulsed by volley fire (2b). Reforming its line, the Erie County militia is reinforced by the Genesee County Militia (2c) and an artillery piece (2d). Together they form a line and block the road, stalling the British advance.

3. American reinforcements of mounted infantry (3), under Colonel Chapin, arrive from Buffalo. Colonel Chapin demands an immediate attack be made on the British position by the county militias.

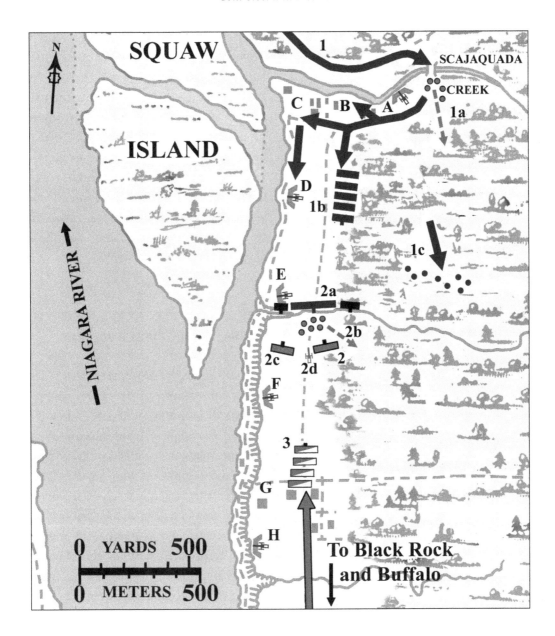

AMERICAN MILITIA FORCES, BLACK ROCK–BUFFALO, DECEMBER 27–29, 1813[3]

Black Rock (Brigadier General Hopkins)
Erie County Militia (Lieutenant Colonel Warren), 150 other ranks
Clarence County Militia (Major Hill), 80 other ranks
Genesee County Militia (Lieutenant Colonel Churchill), 150 other ranks
State Militia Cavalry (Captain Ransom), 37 troopers
Native allies (Lieutenant Colonel Granger), 83 warriors
Artillery (Lieutenant Seeley), 25 gunners with 4 cannon
Chautaqua Militia (Lieutenant Colonel McMahan), 300 other ranks (joined on December 29th)

Buffalo (Major General Hall)
Ontario County Militia (Lieutenant Colonel Blakeslee), 433 other ranks
Genesee County Militia (Major Adams), 382 other ranks
Buffalo Militia (Lieutenant Colonel Chapin), 136 other ranks
Canadian Volunteers (Lieutenant Colonel Mallory), 97 other ranks
Mounted Volunteers (Lieutenant Colonel Broughton), 129 troopers
Artillery (Major Dudley), 100 gunners with 4 cannon

had a clear field of fire across to Fort Erie with eleven heavy cannon and one mortar. An additional mobile battery of four guns covered the land approach to Buffalo, while cavalry pickets roamed the outlying areas, watching for signs of enemy movement. Hall's ground forces consisted of some 2,000 militia plus detachments of regulars, spare artillery crews, and seamen from the four sailing vessels wintering in the dockyard, in all around 2,500 men.[3] Unfortunately in Hall's own words these troops were "disorganized and confused and everything wore the appearance of consternation and dismay."[4]

THE ASSAULT ON BLACK ROCK AND BUFFALO, DECEMBER 29, 1813

On the evening of December 29, 1813, the British boats were moved up from the Chippawa to the embarkation point, four miles below Fort Erie. Around midnight the initial crossing took place without incident or detection. Moving quickly forward, the Light Company of the 89th Regiment captured the Scajaquada Creek Bridge picket, the nearby navy yard, and the "Sailor's" battery (so called because it was manned by men taken from vessels trapped in port for the winter) after only a short fight. Securing the bridge, they were then forced to halt to await the arrival of the remainder

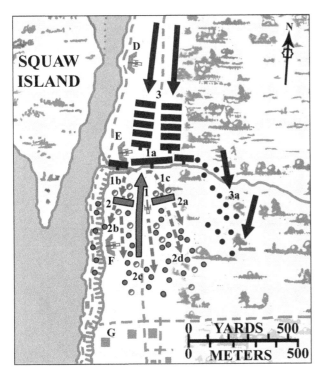

CHAPIN'S ATTACK IS ROUTED

D. The "Sailor's" battery
E. Fieldwork battery
F. "Swift's" battery
G. Brigadier General Porter's house

1. Colonel Chapin leads his cavalry (1) forward, intending to make a surprise attack, but instead blunders into heavy fire from the strong British line (1a). The cavalry rout (1b, 1c), fleeing back through the following infantry, precipitating a cascade collapse and rout of the militia regiments (2b, 2c, 2d).

3. Additional British reinforcements arrive from the beachhead (3), while detachments of Native allies (3a) infiltrate and press around the American position, harassing the fleeing American troops.

of their force, as the ice floes on the river were slowing down the passage and landing of the follow-up waves. Meanwhile, upriver at Buffalo, once the alarm had been raised, the militia companies had fallen in upon their respective parades, ready for action. However, a complete breakdown of communications and leadership left the men standing around in the freezing cold for over two hours before the first detachments were ordered to march from Buffalo for Black Rock, while the remainder

of the troops stayed behind and continued to freeze for nearly two more hours. Leading the way, Lieutenant Colonel Warren moved his Erie County Militia past Black Rock without opposition, but soon ran headlong into the main British force, losing his entire advance guard to enemy fire. Recoiling, Warren blocked the main road and established a line of defence that was soon reinforced by Lieutenant Colonel Churchill's Genesee County Militia and a single artillery piece.

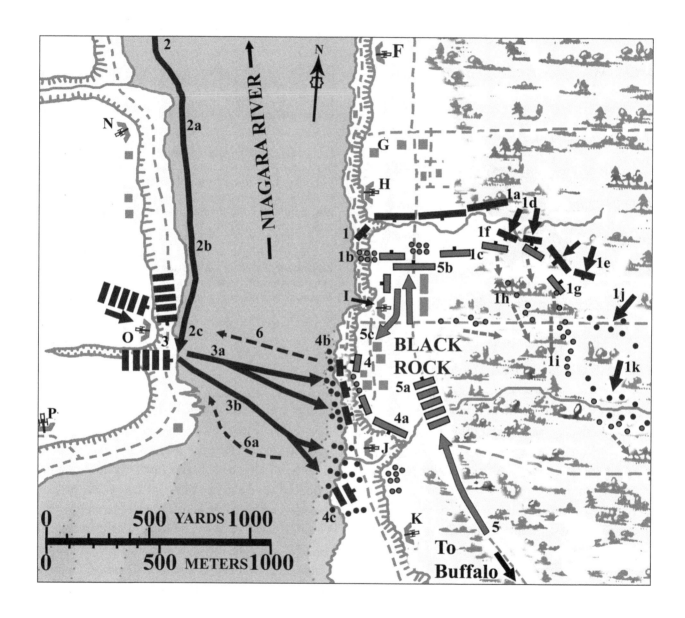

THE BRITISH SECOND LANDING

American

F.   "Swift's" battery
G.   Brigadier General Porter's house
H.   "Dudley's" battery
I.   "Fort Tompkins"
J.   "Old Sow" battery
K.   "Upper" river battery

British

N.   The "Red House" battery
O.   The "Ferry" battery
P.   "No. 1" river battery

1. The British right flank (1, 1a) maintains a steady pressure on the remaining American forces (1b, 1c) defending the riverside road. At the same time the British left flank (1d, 1e) repeatedly manoeuvre around and outflank the American right flank (1f, 1g), precipitating a series of collapses and routs of the dwindling American force (1h, 1i). On the far left flank Native allies (1j, 1k) continue to infiltrate and harass the retreating American troops.

2. Previously delayed in the loading and transportation of the successive waves of troops involved in the initial landings (off map), the boats (2) finally begin their movement upriver. However, they encounter difficulties by repeatedly running aground (2a, 2b), due to low water levels. After a strenuous effort, the boats are freed and arrive at the second embarkation point near the ferry dock (2c).

3. The first wave of the waiting British/Canadian/Native allied troops (3) are loaded into the boats, but with daylight are fully exposed as they begin their crossing (3a, 3b).

4. The American batteries (I, J, K) and infantry (4, 4a) at Black Rock begin firing on the approaching wave of British boats, inflicting casualties. The boats run aground while still offshore, forcing the attackers to wade ashore (4b, 4c) before reforming and pressing their attack.

5. The Ontario County Militia (5) under Lieutenant Colonel Blakeslee, arrives from Buffalo and advances (5a) directly to support the units holding the main road. Forming line (5b), his unit then receives word to withdraw and reposition (5c) in support of the troops at the riverbank facing the second British landing.

6. The British boats repeatedly return across the river (6, 6a) to pick up and ferry successive waves of troops for this flank's attack.

Effectively blocking the British advance, Warren and Churchill were surprised when Lieutenant Colonel Chapin arrived with a large detachment of mounted infantrymen and began berating them for remaining on the defensive and demanding that an immediate counterattack be made. Despite the darkness, and without making any reconnaissance of the enemy's positions, Chapin personally led the advance. Within moments the horsemen blundered into the British line, receiving a volley of musketry at point-blank range for their recklessness. Again led by Chapin, the militia cavalry broke and stampeded back through Warren and Churchill's lines. The result was inevitable, as the panicked cavalry

THE AMERICAN FORCES RETREAT TOWARD BUFFALO

H. "Dudley's" battery
I. "Fort Tompkins"
J. "Old Sow" battery
K. "Upper" river battery

1. British forces from the beachhead (1, 1a) link up with the land attack (1b, 1c), while additional troops are ferried across from Fort Erie (1d, 1e) and advance (1f, 1g, 1h) to support the front line.

2. American resolution crumbles as some units rout while others make a more orderly retreat (2, 2a, 2b, 2c, 2d).

3. British Native allied detachments (3), having penetrated to the rear of the American forces, continue their harassment of the Americans all the way into Buffalo.

set off a cascading rout within the infantry. Little in the way of an organized defence was now left to hold back the fully reinforced assault force, and the British moved forward toward the intended site of the second landing, opposed only by parts of companies and detachments of men who rallied around any officer who stood his ground.

Elsewhere, the British plan of assault was not proceeding smoothly. The initial landings had taken longer than anticipated and whilst moving upriver to collect the second assault force, many boats ran aground due to low water levels in the ice-clogged river. The only solution was for the crews to climb out of the boats and wade waist deep in the frigid water to physically manhandle the boats past the shoals and into deeper water, where they could then reach the designated embarkation point, all the while maintaining the strictest silence as they were "under the point blank fire of the enemy's heaviest batteries."[5] By the time these problems had been overcome and the boats had been loaded with troops, dawn had arrived, allowing the Americans to see the intended attack wave coming and open fire. Under heavy artillery bombardment and then volleys of musketry as they neared the shoreline, the men in the boats suffered a growing number of casualties, while only being able to reply with an intermittent fire from the crowded vessels. As they approached the American shoreline, the low water levels grounded many of the boats on a line of rocks, well away from the bank of the river. Unable to get closer, the troops were forced to wade ashore, carrying their weapons and cartridge boxes over their heads, before forming up — soaking wet and freezing cold — to engage the American force before them.

For General Hall this second assault was a crisis capping a series of setbacks that began as soon as the news of the first British landing had reached him at Buffalo. Getting initial reports from Warren that the forces at Black Rock were holding their positions, he had dispatched the remaining detachments of Genesee Militia, under Major Adams, to reinforce that flank. Unfortunately, as the column moved forward they came across Chapin's cavalrymen hurrying to the rear, bringing tales of large numbers of Natives and British regulars crushing all opposition. Within a half hour desertion from the column had eroded it to nothing, leaving the few detachments of Americans still putting up resistance beyond Black Rock in a desperate position as the redcoats and Natives pressed their advantage by infiltrating to the rear and forcing the defenders to retreat or risk capture. News of this

British advance soon spread throughout Buffalo, and numerous men, seeing no hope of success, deserted directly from their parades and regimental barracks, leaving behind their weapons and accoutrements. Hall now had no choice but to send his only remaining intact regiment — Lieutenant Colonel Blakeslee's Ontario County Militia as a final force to oppose Riall's advance, while Hall remained in Buffalo to gather up what remained of his reserves and advance them toward Black Rock. Passing the batteries at Black Rock, Blakeslee's force of around 430 men soon came in contact with the enemy, whereupon he formed his line-of-battle and was prepared to launch an immediate attack with the bayonet. Instead, after consulting with his second-in-command, Major Gardener, Blakeslee was persuaded to await the coming daybreak before ordering an attack. Shortly thereafter the sound of heavy gunfire came from his rear at the Black Rock batteries, and within moments a dispatch arrived from General Hall, recalling Blakeslee's force to Black Rock.

Expecting to join Blakeslee and fight the British advancing along the main road, Hall had brought up the remaining reinforcements to Black Rock just as the riverside batteries began firing at the approaching final assault wave of British boats. Realizing he was being caught in a vice, Hall immediately sent for Blakeslee's Ontario

ESTIMATES OF CASUALTIES, BLACK ROCK-BUFFALO, DECEMBER 29, 1813[9, 10]

American

By General Hall's Report

Killed:	est. 32 all ranks
Wounded:	est. 40 all ranks,
Missing and Prisoners:	est. 53 all ranks

By Independent Accounts

Killed:	minimum 50 all ranks
Wounded:	minimum 52 all ranks
Missing and Prisoners:	minimum 100 all ranks

British

British Regulars

Killed:	25 rank and file
Wounded:	1 officer, 3 sergeants, 57 rank and file
Missing:	9 rank and file

Canadian Militia

Killed:	5 rank and file
Wounded:	5 rank and file

Native Allies

Killed:	3 warriors
Wounded:	3 warriors

County Militia to support the guns and hopefully fend off the amphibious wave while he went to support Warren's and Churchill's depleted force facing Riall's ever-encroaching land attack. After an initial resistance of around twenty minutes — as the second British force continued to enlarge its beachhead — the riverside batteries were eventually overrun, forcing the Americans to retire inland. At the same time, the first British force finally succeeded in pushing aside Churchill's wavering militia and hit Blakeslee's retreating force in the flank, precipitating a complete collapse of all the American forces and a rout that soon ended up in Buffalo proper. Deciding that the battle was lost, Hall and his staff abandoned their headquarters and left the field, while the British and Natives steadily advanced, harassed only by isolated pockets of resistance until they reached a small fortified battery covering the main road leading into the town. This well-prepared position could have provided a focus for a final defence of Buffalo, but with no effective leadership few troops were prepared to make a stand. After firing a few desultory rounds from a dilapidated canon, the position was taken in the first British rush, as later reported by General Riall in his account to General Drummond: "He [the Americans] here shewed a large body of Infantry and Cavalry and attempted to oppose our advance by the fire of a field piece posted on a height which commanded the road. But finding this ineffectual, he fled in all directions and betaking himself to the woods — further pursuit was useless...."[6]

Nor was the defence of the town given much credit in later accounts by at least one civilian eye-witness, a Mrs. Olivia Mitchell from Black Rock:

We ... had such confidence in numbers that we thought there was no doubt our troops could defend us. But alas! We found when too late that militia wouldn't stand fire in the dark but took to the woods, where the Indians outflanked them and many, very many, met their death there. Many more got away, while only a small body retreated to Buffalo.... When we got into the village [Buffalo] there was such confusion about the public houses, drums beating to arms, officers riding about giving orders, etc. etc.... When we got to the [lakeshore] road that comes out of the woods by Granger's Creek, it was broad daylight.... But the road was filled literally from one fence to the other, and they kept accumu-lating, for the panic was so great ... that the people left their houses all the way as we went along ... a great many of them driving their cattle, sheep and hogs; all running away from comfortable homes; little children drawn on sleds and in baby wagons. When we got to Williamsville we found a guard on the bridge to keep the militia from crossing, but that made no difference, they would wade the creek, for they were so frightened they could not stop running. [7]

General Hall and the remnants of the American force on the Niagara subsequently retreated from Buffalo to their own Eleven Mile Creek. In the days that followed, in an attempt to exonerate himself for this defeat, Major General Hall wrote to Governor Tompkins, blaming the American Native allies and militia for not standing firm, and claiming that his losses were relatively light at thirty-two killed, forty wounded, and fifty-three prisoners.[8] However, other reports cast significant doubt upon this claim, lending credibility to the British version of the affair whereby, in addition to 279 recorded prisoners, the American toll of killed and wounded could have reached beyond 300. [*9, *10]

Having completely dispersed his enemy, General Riall accepted the surrender of the village from Colonel Chapin and then undertook the secondary

153

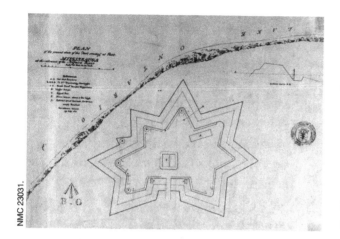

NMC 23031.

The plan for the construction of Fort Mississauga, 1813–14.

A modern, but still chilling, wintry view of Fort Mississauga

of four vessels. In a similar fashion, many civilian homes at Buffalo, as well as the Seneca Native village, were looted (although the evidence of some American eyewitnesses point toward elements of the retreating American troops as an equal culprit of this crime)[11] before being put to the torch, leaving a wasteland of ashes behind when the British withdrew to their own side of the river a few days later.

For all practical purposes, the American Niagara frontier was now entirely defenceless and the panic of the troops at Buffalo spread amongst the surrounding counties of western New York, causing many families to abandon their homes and farms and flee to the interior of the state. This caused Governor Tompkins to send urgent pleas to Secretary of War Armstrong to immediately dispatch regular troops from their winter quarters at French Mills for the defence of the Niagara.

On the other side of the river, the burning of Newark had been revenged tenfold. Furthermore, following the capture of Fort Niagara, construction of a new fortification (Fort Mississauga) was begun on the western bank to entirely close of the mouth of the Niagara River to American traffic. Ironically, this fort's main tower was partially built using scavenged bricks from the gutted buildings of Newark.

However, while the frontier was temporarily secure, the fact remained that the regular regiments in Upper Canada had been used almost to the point

purpose of his expedition by carrying off everything that the Buffalo military warehouses contained and razing all the remaining magazines, warehouses, barracks, and defences at Buffalo and Black Rock, as well as the important dockyard and its contents of extinction, and without reinforcements or replacement units, General Drummond was certain that any new American offensive in the spring would succeed by sheer weight of numbers. Furthermore, the essential foundation of agricultural production had been effectively ruined along the Niagara frontier and hungry times were in store for the military, civilian, and Native populations alike — unless Drummond could extract an increased supply of materiel from the ever-reluctant Sir George Prevost.

From the American perspective, by the end of 1813 the state of affairs was so bad that on December 31st the American House of Representatives established a Congressional committee of inquiry "requesting such information (not improper to be communicated) as may tend to explain the causes of the failure of the arms of the United States on the Northern frontier …"[12] from Secretary of War, John Armstrong.

In a fifty-page printed report submitted a month later, Armstrong responded with a detailed series of transcripts and copies of letters and reports, all relating to the military debacles of the previous months. On the other hand, the report failed to present any conclusions or recommendations as to how these failures could be remedied. Instead, it was left to the details provided by the letters within the report to tell their own story of the cause of the American humiliations that had been suffered on the field of battle.

Reviewing the last half of the year, Upper Canada seemed to have, by some miracle, once more been preserved. However, the United States had achieved one of its main war aims by effectively neutralizing the vast potential of the western Native nations as a source of manpower for the British war effort and eliminated their greatest individual threat through the death of Tecumseh. They had also ended British military control of Lake Erie and the Detroit frontier. In addition, politically the British government had reconsidered its pre-war arrogant policies toward the Americans and was now actively prepared to undertake peace negotiations. Finally, within the American military system the doddering and incompetent strata of senior American generals had almost all been removed from office by the calamities of the previous year, and a new breed of younger, experienced, competent, and aggressive commanders had emerged. These new leaders were hardened in battle and, if nothing else, were certain of how *not* to conduct a campaign. Furthermore, below them most of the individual regimental commanders and even the rank and file of the regular forces were veterans of the battlefield. All that was wanting was the opportunity to bring all this experience together so that a new American army could be born from the humiliations of 1813.

That story will be recounted in the next book in this series, *The Tide of War.*

NOTES

A star indicates the note refers to a sidebar.

ABBREVIATIONS:

LAC: Library and Archives of Canada.
AOO: Archives of Ontario.
CRDH: Ernest Cruikshank, *The Documentary History of the Campaigns upon the Niagara Frontier 1812–1814*, 9 Volumes (Welland, ON: Tribune Press, 1896–1908).
CGMC: Buffalo and Erie County Historical Society Archives, B00-11, A. Conger Goodyear War of 1812 Manuscripts, 1779–1862.
SBD1812: William C.H. Wood, *Select British Documents of the War of 1812* (Toronto: Champlain Society of Canada, 1920).

CHAPTER 2: STRIKING WHILE THE IRON IS HOT: THE NIAGARA FRONTIER, JULY–AUGUST 1813

1.   LAC, RG8-I: British Military and Naval Records, 1757–1903, Vol. 679, 187.
*2.   LAC, RG8-I: British Military and Naval Records, 1757–1903, Vol. 1219, 84; CGMC, Vol. 5; CRDC, Vol. 6, 127.
*3.   H. Perry Smith, ed., *History of the City of Buffalo & Erie Country*, Vol. 1 (Syracuse NY: D. Mason & Co, 1884), 140–41.
4.   CGMC, Vol. 5; Klinck, *Journal of Major John Norton*, Publication No. 46, 327.
*5.   LAC, RG8-I: British Military and Naval Records, 1757–1903, Vol. 1, 219, 85, and Vol. 679, 231; CRDC, Vol. 6, 216, 227, 233; *History of the City of Buffalo and Erie County*, Vol. 1, 141–44.
6.   *Utica Patriot*, August 24, 1813.
7.   CRDC, Vol. 6, 204.
8.   Kirby Papers, Detroit Public Library Archives.
9.   Edgar Ridout, Lady Matilda, and Thomas Ridout, *Ten Years in Upper Canada in Peace & War, 1805–1815. Being the Ridout Letters with Annotations by Matilda Edgar* (Toronto: William Brigs, 1890), 204.

10. CRDC, Vol. 6, 207–08.

11. J.P. Boyd, *Documents and Facts Relative to Military Events During the Late War* (Private Publishing, 1816), 18. General Boyd to Secretary of War Armstrong, August 16, 1813.

12. *Journal of Major John Norton*, Publication No. 46, 338.

13. Ernest Cruikshank, *The Blockade of Fort George, 1813* (Niagara Historical Society Papers, No. 3, 1898), 42–44.

14. SBD1812, Vol. 2, 185–86.

15. *Ibid.*

CHAPTER 3: GOING FROM BAD TO WORSE: THE DETROIT FRONTIER, JULY–AUGUST 1813

1. Sandy Antal, *A Wampum Denied: Proctor's War of 1812* (Ottawa: Carleton University Press, 1997), 254.

2. *Ibid.*, 259.

CHAPTER 4: MOVE AND COUNTER MOVE: AUGUST–SEPTEMBER 1813

1. C. Chapin, *Chapin's Review of Armstrong's Notices of the War of 1812* (Black Rock, NY: Private Publication, 1836), 198–200.

2. Cruikshank, *The Blockade of Fort George, 1813* (Niagara Historical Society Papers, No. 3, 1898).

3. *Ibid.*

4. *Ibid.*

5. LAC, RG8-I: British Military and Naval Records, 1757–1903, Vol. 680, 68–70.

CHAPTER 5: THE VICE BEGINS TO TIGHTEN: THE DETROIT FRONTIER, SEPTEMBER 1813

1. Antal, *A Wampum Denied*, 281–82.

*2. Robert Malcomson, *Warships of the Great Lakes 1754–1834* (Rochester, UK: Chatham Publishing, 2001), 88.

*3. *Ibid.*

4. LAC, RG8-I: British Military and Naval Records, 1757–1903, Vol. 731, 116.

CHAPTER 6: THE VICE CLOSES

1. Antal, *A Wampum Denied*, 315.

2. *Ibid.*, 316.

3. *Ibid.*, 317.

4. *Ibid.*, 317.

CHAPTER 7: A CRUSHING DEFEAT

1. Antal, *A Wampum Denied*, 336–37; Casselman, ed., *Richardson's War of 1812*, Vol. 1, 218, 234; G. Stott, *Greater Evils: The War of 1812 in Southwestern Ontario* (Self-published, 2001), 60–62; Sandy Antal, *Invasions: Taking and Retaking Detroit and the Western District during the War of 1812 and its Aftermath* (Essex, ON: Essex County Historical Society, 2011), 37.

2. *Ibid.*

*3. Casselman, ed., *Richardson's War of 1812*, Vol. 1, 230–33.

4. *Ibid.*, 232–33; David Lomax, *A History of the Service of the 41st (the Welch) Regiment* (Davenport, UK: Hiorns & Miller, 1899), 111–12.

*5. Antal, *A Wampum Denied*, 347–48; Casselman, ed., *Richardson's War of 1812*, Vol. 1, 218, 234; Stott, *Greater Evils*, 64–66.

CHAPTER 8: HARD CHOICES

1. Casselman, ed., *Richardson's War of 1812*, Vol. 1, 219.

2. LAC, RG8-I: British Military and Naval Records, 1757–1903, Vol. 680, 68–70.

CHAPTER 9: SEESAW ON THE NIAGARA: OCTOBER–NOVEMBER 1813

1. Government of the United States, *Causes of the Failure of the Army on the Northern Frontier,* Report to the House of Representatives February 2, 1814; 13th Congress, 2nd Session, Military Affairs, Vol. 1, 482; J. Brannan, *Official Letters of the Military and Naval Officers of the United States, during the War with Great Britain in the Years 1812, 13, 14, & 15* (Washington, DC: Way & Gideon, 1823), 242.
2. CRDH, Vol. 9, 121.
3. Major John Kearsley, "The Memoirs of Major John Kearsley: A Michigan Hero from the War of 1812," *Military History Journal* 10 (May 1985). Clement Library, University of Michigan.
4. Government of the United States, *Causes of the Failure of the Army on the Northern Frontier,* Vol. 1, 484–85; Brannan, *Official Letters of the Military and Naval Officers of the United States,* 269–70.
*5. LAC, RG8-I: British Military and Naval Records, 1757–1903, Vol. 681, 237.
6. *Illustrated Historical Atlas of the Counties of Lincoln and Welland* (Toronto: H.R. Page, 1876), 9. Unidentified British Officer at Niagara, December 1813.

CHAPTER 10: THE ST. LAWRENCE CAMPAIGN: SEPTEMBER–NOVEMBER 1813

1. LAC, Duncan Clark Papers, MG19, A39, Vol. 3, 129.
2. *Ibid.,* 139.
3. John Kilborn, "Accounts of the War of 1812," in T.H.W. Leavitt, *History of Leeds and Grenville Counties from 1749 to 1879* (Brockville, ON: Recorder Press, 1879), 36.
*4. Donald Graves, *Field of Glory: The Battle of Crysler's arm 1813* (Toronto: Robin Brass Studio, 1999), 362.
*5. *Ibid.*
6. J.L. Thomson, *Historical Sketches of the Late War Between the United States and Great Britain* (Philadelphia: Thomas Delsilver, 1816), 183.

7. G. Auchinleck, *A History of the War between Great Britain and the United States of America during the years 1812, 1813 & 1814* (Originally published 1853 by Thomas Maclear. Reprint Published 1972 Arms & Armour Press and Pendragon House), 251.

CHAPTER 11: THE BATTLE OF CRYSLER'S FARM: NOVEMBER 11, 1813

*1. Donald Graves, *Field of Glory: The Battle of Crysler's Farm 1813* (Toronto: Robin Brass Studio, 1999), 360–61; Ronald L. Way, *The Day of Crysler's Farm* (Morrisburg, ON: The Ontario-St. Lawrence Development Commission, No Date), 20–30.
*2. Graves, *Field of Glory,* 268–72; Way, *The Day of Crysler's Farm,* 20–30.

CHAPTER 12: A NEW BROOM

1. CRDH, Vol. 8, 271–72 (December 12, 1813).
*2. Government of the United States, *Causes of the Failure of the Army on the Northern Frontier,* Vol. 1, 487–48.
3. SBD1812, Vol. 2, 485–86; LAC, RG8-I: British Military and Naval Records, 1757–1903, Vol. 681, 258.
4. *Ibid.*
*5. LAC, RG8-I: British Military and Naval Records, 1757–1903, Vol. 681, 244–49.
*6. *Ibid.,* 250; LAC, RG8-I: British Military and Naval Records, 1757–1903, Vol. 1219, 179.

CHAPTER 13: FLAMES ALONG THE BORDER: THE NIAGARA FRONTIER, DECEMBER 1813

1. LAC, RG8-I: British Military and Naval Records, 1757–1903, Vol. 681, 264.
2. Niagara Historical Society Papers, No. 30, letter from Dr. Lorey (8th [Kings] Regiment) to Lieutenant S.H.P. Graves (9th Regiment).

3. CRDH, Vol. 9, 24.

4. *Ibid.*, 52.

5. *Ibid.*, 54.

CHAPTER 14: COLD STEEL AND HOT FIRE

1. LAC, RG8-I: British Military and Naval Records, 1757–1903, Vol. 681, 310.

*2. LAC, RG8-I: British Military and Naval Records, 1757–1903, Vol. 682, 5.

*3. Smith, ed., *History of the City of Buffalo & Erie Country*, Vol. 1, 148.

4. LAC, RG8-I: British Military and Naval Records, 1757–1903, Vol. 1219, 181.

5. *Ibid.*

6. LAC, RG8-I: British Military and Naval Records, 1757–1903, Vol. 682, 5–7.

7. Journal of Mrs. Olivia Mitchell, *Buffalo Courier*, January 11, 1881.

8. CRDH, Vol. 9, 91.

*9 W. Jay, "Table of the Killed and Wounded in the War of 1812" (Ithaca, NY: New York State Historical Monographs, Historical Literature Collection, Cornell University Library).

*10. LAC, RG8-I: British Military and Naval Records, 1757–1903, Vol. 1219, 185; LAC, RG8-I: British Military and Naval Records, 1757–1903, Vol. 682, 11.

11. CRDH, Vol. 9, 64; Carl Benn, *The Iroquois in the War of 1812* (Toronto: University of Toronto Press, 1998), 15.

12. Government of the United States, *Causes of the Failure of the Army on the Northern Frontier*, Vol. 1.

SELECTED BIBLIOGRAPHY

PRIMARY SOURCES

Archival

1. Library and Archives of Canada
   Manuscript Groups (MG)
   MG10A: U.S. Department of State, War of 1812 Records
   MG11 (CO42): British Colonial Office, Original Correspondence, Canada
   MG11 (CO47): Upper Canada Records, 1764–1836, Miscellaneous
   MG13 (WO62): Commissariat Dept, Miscellaneous Records 1809–1814
   MG19/A39: Duncan Clark Papers
   MG24/A9: Sir George Prevost Papers

   Research Groups (RG)
   RG5-A1: Civil Secretary's Office, Upper Canada Sundries, 1791–1867
   RG8-I: British Military and Naval Records, 1757–1903
   RG9-I: Pre-Confederation Records, Military
   RG10: Indian Department Records
   RG19/E5A: Department of Finance, War of 1812, Losses Board

2. Archives Ontario
   MS35/1: Strachan Papers
   MS74/R5: Merritt Papers
   MS501: Thorburn Papers
   MS58: Band Papers
   MS500: Street Papers
   MS519: Joel Stone Papers
   MS520: Solomon Jones Papers
   MS502/B Series: Nelles Papers
   MU2099: A.A. Rapelje Papers
   MU527: Duncan Clark Papers
   MU2034: Events in the Military History of the Saint Lawrence River Valley 1779–1814
   MS74.R5: Henry Ruttan Papers
   Microfilm B91/Reel 1: Table of Statutes, Upper Canada Legislature 1792–1840

3. Metro Toronto Reference Library
   Hagerman, C.: Journal of Christopher Hagerman

MacDonell, G.: MacDonell Papers
Prevost Papers, 7 Vols., S108, Cub 7

4. Detroit Public Library Archives
Kirby, J.: James Kirby Papers

5. Buffalo and Erie County Historical Society Archives, A. Conger Goodyear War of 1812 Manuscripts, 1779–1862, Mss. BOO-11, 16 Volumes

EARLY SECONDARY PUBLICATIONS

Armstrong, J. *Notices of the War of 1812*. New York: Wiley & Putnam, 1840.

Boyd, J.P. *Documents and Facts Relative to Military Events during the Late War*. Private publication, 1816.

Brackenridge, Henry. M. *History of the Late War between the United States and Great Britain*. Cushing & Jewett, 1817.

Brannan, J. *Official Letters of the Military and Naval Officers of the United States, during the War with Great Britain in the Years 1812, 13, 14, & 15*.Washington, DC: Way & Gideon, 1823.

Chapin, C. *Chapin's Review of Armstrong's Notices of the War of 1812*. Black Rock, NY: Private publication, 1836.

Davis, Paris M. *An Authentick History of the Late War between the United States and Great Britain*. Ithica, NY: Mack & Andrus, 1829.

_____. *The Four Principal Battles of the Late War between the United States and Great Britain*. Harrisburg, NY: Jacob Baab, 1832.

Dawson, M. *A Historical Narrative of the True Civil and Military Services of Major-General William H. Harrison*. Cincinnati: *Cincinnati Advertiser*, 1824.

Dearborn, H.A.S. *Defence of Gen. Henry Dearborn, Against the Attack of Gen. William Hull*. Boston: E.W. Davies, 1824.

Gilleland, J.C. *History of the Late War between the United States and Great Britain*. Baltimore: Schaeffer & Maund, 1817.

Hitsman, J.M. *History of the American War of Eighteen Hundred and Twelve*. Philadelphia: W. McCarty, 1816.

Izard, George. *Official Correspondence with the Department of War Relative to the Military Operations of the American Army Under the Command of Major General Izard of the Northern Frontier of the United States in the Years 1814 and 1815*. Philadelphia: Thomas Dobson, 1816.

James, W. *A Full and Correct Account of the Military Occurrences of the Late War between Great Britain and the United States of America*. London: William James, 1818.

McCarty, W. *History of the American War of 1812*. Philadelphia: William McCarty & Davis, 1817.

Merritt, William Hamilton. *Journal of Events: Principally on the Detroit and Niagara Frontiers during the War of 1812*. St. Catharines, ON: Canada West Historical Society, 1863.

Morgan, J.C. *The Emigrant's Guide, with Recollections of Upper and Lower Canada during the Late War between the United States of America and Great Britain*. London: Longman, Hurst, Rees, Orme & Brown, 1824.

O'Connor, T. *An Impartial and Correct History of the War between the United States of America and Great Britain*. Belfast: Joseph Smyth, 1816. Reprint of the John Low edition, New York, 1815.

Perkins, S. *A History of the Political and Military Events of the Late War between the United States and Great Britain*. New Haven, CT: S. Converse, 1825.

"Proceedings and Debates of the House of Representatives of the United States." 12th Congress, 1st Session (1812). U.S. Government Records.

Ripley, E.A. *Facts Relative to the Campaign on the Niagara in 1814*. Boston: Self-published, 1815.

Thomson, J.L. *Historical Sketches of the Late War between the United States and Great Britain*. Philadelphia: Thomas Delsilver, 1816.

United States Congress. *Barbarities of the Enemy Exposed in a report of the Committee of the House of Representatives of the United States*. Worcester, MA: Isaac Sturtevant, 1814.

Wilkinson, J. *Diagrams and Plans Illustrative of the Principal Battles of the War of 1812*. Philadelphia: Self-published, 1815.

SECONDARY SOURCES

Later Secondary Publications

Baylies, N. *Eleazar Wheellock Ripley of the War of 1812.* Des Moine, IA: Brewster & Co., 1890.

Blakeslee, S. *Narrative of Colonel Samuel Blakeslee: A Defender of Buffalo in the War of 1812.* Buffalo, NY: Buffalo Historical Society Publications, 1905.

Buell, W. "Military Movements in Eastern Ontario during the War of 1812." *Ontario Historical Society, Papers and Records,* Vol. 10 (1913) and Vol. 17 (1919).

Cannon, R.J. *Historical Records of the British Army: The First, or, Royal Regiment of Foot.* London, UK: William Clowes and Sons, 1847.

_____. *Historical Record of the Eighth, or, the Kings Regiment of Foot.* London, UK: Parker, Furnival, and Parker, 1844.

Carnochan, Janet. *Reminiscences of Niagara and St. Davids.* Niagara Historical Society, Paper No. 20 (1911).

Crooks, James. "Recollections of the Late Hon. James Crooks." Niagara Historical Society Papers, No. 28, c. 1916.

Cruickshank, Ernest. "A Memoir of Colonel the Honourable James Kerby, His Life in Letters." Welland County Historical Society, Papers and Records, No. 4, 1931.

_____. "The Battle of Fort George." Niagara Historical Society, Paper No. 12 (1912). Reprint by Niagara Historical Society, 1990.

_____. "The Blockade of Fort George." Niagara Historical Society, Paper No. 3.

_____. "Campaigns of 1812–1814." Niagara Historical Society, Paper No. 9, 1902.

_____. "Letters of 1812 from the Dominion Archives." Niagara Historical Society, Paper No. 23, 1913.

Dorsheimer, W. "The Village of Buffalo during the War of 1812." Presentation to the Buffalo Historical Society, 1863.

Edgar, M. and Thomas Ridout. *Ten Years in Upper Canada in Peace & War, 1805–1815: Being the Ridout Letters with Annotations by Matilda Edgar.* Toronto: William Brigs, 1890.

"Family History and Reminiscences of Early Settlers and Recollections of the War of 1812." Niagara Historical Society, Paper No. 28, 1915.

Government of the United States. *Causes of the Failure of the Army on the Northern Frontier.* Report to the House of Representatives, February 2, 1814, 13th Congress, 2nd Session, Military Affairs.

"Historic Houses." Niagara Historical Society, Paper No. 5, 1899.

Johnson, Frederick H. *A Guide for Every Visitor to Niagara Falls.* Buffalo, NY: Phinney & Co., 1852.

"Journal of Mrs. Olivia Mitchell, Read before the Buffalo Historical Society January 10, 1881." Extract from the *Buffalo Courier,* January 11, 1881.

Kearsley, Major J. "The Memoirs of Major John Kearsley: A Michigan Hero from the War of 1812." *Military History Journal* 10 (May 1985). Clement Library, University of Michigan.

Kilborn, John. "Accounts of the War of 1812." In, Thaddeus W.H. Leavitt. *History of Leeds and Grenville Counties from 1749 to 1879.* Brockville, ON: Recorder Press, 1879.

Leavitt, T.W.H. *History of Leeds and Grenville Counties from 1749 to 1879.* Brockville, ON: Recorder Press, 1879.

Lossing, Benson. *Pictorial Field Book of the War of 1812.* New York: Harper and Brothers, 1868.

"Reminiscences of Arthur Galloway." Ithaca, NY: Cornell University Library.

"Reminiscences of Niagara." Niagara Historical Society, Paper No. 11 (1904).

Scott, Winfield. *Memoirs of Lieut. General Scott.* New York: Sheldon & Co., 1864.

Severence, F.H., ed. *The Case of Brigadier General Alexander Smyth.* Buffalo Historical Society Publications, 18, (1941).

_____. *Papers Relating to the War of 1812 on the Niagara Frontier.* Buffalo Historical Society Publications, No. 5 (1902).

Smith, H. Perry, ed. *History of the City of Buffalo & Erie Country.* Vol. 1. Syracuse, NY: D. Mason & Co, 1884.

State Historical Monographs, Historical Literature Collection, Anonymous collection, circa 1850.

Warner, Robert I. *Memoirs of Capt. John Lampman and His Wife Mary Secord*. Welland County Historical Society, Papers and Records (1927), 3, 126–34.

Wright, Ross Pier. *The Burning of Dover*. Unpublished manuscript (1948).

Books

Adams, Henry. *History of the United States of America during the Administrations of Madison*. New York: Library of America, 1986. Reprint of original 1891 volumes.

Antal, Sandy. *A Wampum Denied, Proctor's War of 1812*. Ottawa: Carleton University Press, 1997.

_____. *Invasions, Taking and Retaking Detroit and the Western District during the War of 1812*. Essex County Historical Society, 2011.

Auchinleck, George. *A History of the War between Great Britain and the United States of America during the Years 1812, 1813 & 1814*. Toronto: Thomas Maclear, 1853. Reprint by Arms & Armour Press and Pendragon House, 1972.

Babcock, Louis L. *The War of 1812 on the Niagara Frontier*. Volume 29. Buffalo, NY: Buffalo Historical Society Publications, 1927.

Benn, Carl. *The Iroquois in the War of 1812*. Toronto: University of Toronto Press, 1998.

Bingham, Robert W. *The Cradle of the Queen City: A History of Buffalo to the Incorporation of the City*. Volume 31. Buffalo, NY: Buffalo Historical Society Publications, 1931.

Bowler, R. Arthur, ed. *Essays on the War of 1812 and its Legacy*. Youngstown, NY: Old Fort Niagara Association, 1991.

Brant, Irving. *The Fourth President: A Life of James Madison*. Indianapolis & New York: The Bobbs Merrill Company, 1970.

Casselman, Alexander C., ed. *Richardson's War of 1812*. Toronto: Historical Publishing Co., 1902. Facsimile edition by Coles Publishing Co., Toronto, 1974.

Contest for the Command of Lake Ontario in 1812 & 1813. Transactions of the Royal Society of Canada, SEC II, Series III, Vol. X.

Cruikshank, Ernest. *The Documentary History of the Campaigns upon the Niagara Frontier in 1812–1814*. 9 volumes. Welland, ON: Tribune Press, 1896–1908.

Dunnigan, Brian Leigh. *Forts within a Fort, Niagara's Redoubts*. Youngstown, NY: Old Fort Niagara Association Inc., 1989.

_____. *History and Development of Old Fort Niagara*. Youngstown, NY: Old Fort Niagara Association Inc., 1985.

Elliott, C. *Winfield Scott, the Soldier and the Man*. Toronto: The Macmillan Company of Canada, Ltd., 1937.

Gardiner, Robert, ed. *The Naval War of 1812*. London, UK: Caxton Publishing Group, 2001.

Gayler, Hugh J., ed. *Niagara's Changing Landscapes*. Ottawa: Carleton University Press, 1994.

Gourlay, Robert. *Statistical Account of Upper Canada Compiled with a View to a Grand System of Emigration*. 2 Volumes. London, UK: Simpkin and Marshall, 1822. Republished by the Social Science Research Council of Canada, S.R. Publishers Ltd., Johnson Reprint Corp., 1966.

Graves, D.E. *Field of Glory: The Battle of Crysler's Farm, 1813*. Montreal: Robin Brass Studio, 1999.

_____. *Fix Bayonets! A Royal Welch Fusilier at War 1796–1815*. Montreal: Robin Brass Studio, 2006.

Hitsman, J. Mackay. *The Incredible War of 1812: A Military History*. Montreal: Robin Brass Studio, 1999. Revised edition, updated by Donald Graves.

Hobbs, Raymond. *Things are Going on Very Badly: Burlington Heights, The Head of the Lake, and the British Army in the Fall and Winter of 1813*. Self Published, 2002.

Horsman, R. *The Causes of the War of 1812*. New York: A.S. Barnes and Co., 1962.

Hough, Franklin B. *A History of St. Lawrence and Franklin Counties, New York*. Albany, NY: Little & Co., 1853.

Illustrated Historical Atlas of the Counties of Frontenac, Lennox and Addington. Toronto: J.H. Meachan & Co., 1878.

Illustrated Historical Atlas of the Counties of Hastings & Prince Edward. Toronto: H. Belden & Co., 1878.

Illustrated Historical Atlas of the Counties of Lincoln and Welland. Toronto: H.R. Page, 1876.

Illustrated Historical Atlas of the Counties of Northumberland and Durham. Toronto: H. Belden & Co., 1877.

Illustrated Historical Atlas of the Counties of Stormont, Dundas & Glengarry. Toronto: Belden & Co. Toronto, 1879.

Illustrated Historical Atlas of Norfolk County. Toronto: H. Belden & Co., 1877.

Irving, L.H. *Officers of the British Forces in Canada during the War of 1812.* Toronto: Canadian Military Institute, 1908.

Jarvis Papers. Women's Canadian Historical Society of Toronto Papers and Transactions, Transaction No. 5 (1902), 3–9.

Jay, W. *Table of the Killed and Wounded in the War of 1812.* Ithaca, NY: New York State Historical Monographs, Historical Literature Collection, Cornell University Library.

Johnston, Winston. *The Glengarry Light Infantry, 1812–1816: Who Were They and What Did They Do in the War?* Self-published, 2011.

Klinck, Carl F. *Journal of Major John Norton.* Toronto: Champlain Society of Canada, Publication No. 46, 1970.

Mackay, J. *The Incredible War of 1812.* Toronto: University of Toronto, 1965.

Malcomson, Robert. *A Very Brilliant Affair: The Battle of Queenston Heights, 1812.* Montreal: Robin Brass Studio, 2003.

_____. *Lords of the Lake: The Naval War on Lake Ontario, 1812–1814.* Montreal: Robin Brass Studio, 1998.

_____. *Warships of the Great Lakes, 1754–1834.* Rochester, UK: Chatham Publishing, 2001.

Malcomson, Robert and Thomas Malcomson. *HMS Detroit: The Battle for Lake Erie.* St. Catharines, ON: Vanwell Publishing Limited, 1990.

Niagara Historical Society Papers, Numbers 2, 3, 4, 5, 9, 11, 20, 22, 23, 28, 30, 31, 33.

Ruttan, Henry. *Reminiscences of the Hon. Henry Ruttan: Loyalist Narratives from Upper Canada.* Toronto: Champlain Society, 1946.

Stagg, J.C.A. *Mr. Madison's War: Politics, Diplomacy, and Warfare in the Early American Republic 1783–1830.* Princeton, NJ: Princeton University Press, 1983.

Stanley, George F.G. *The War of 1812: Land Operations.* Toronto: Macmillan of Canada and the Canadian War Museum, 1983.

Stott, Glenn. *Greater Evils: The War of 1812 in Southwestern Ontario.* Self-published, 2001.

Wood, William C.H. *Select British Documents of the War of 1812.* 3 volumes. Toronto: Champlain Society of Canada, 1920.

Wright, Ross Pier. *The Burning of Dover.* Erie: Unpublished manuscript, 1948.

INDEX